SOOGDIERE
VAN DIE KRUGERWILDTUIN EN ANDER NASIONALE PARKE

MAMMALS
OF THE KRUGER AND OTHER NATIONAL PARKS

MAMMIFÈRES
DU PARC KRUGER ET DES AUTRES PARCS NATIONAUX

SÄUGETIERE
IM KRUGER NATIONALPARK UND ANDEREN NATIONALPARKS

Die mens kan nie skep nie,
die mens kan nie eers herskep nie,
hy kan slegs bewaar.

Man cannot create,
man cannot even re-create,
he can only conserve.

L'homme ne peut créer.
L'homme ne peut pas même recréer.
Il ne peut que préserver.

Der Mensch kann nicht erschaffen.
Der Mensch kann nicht einmal
wiedererschaffen.
Er kann nur erhalten.

ROCCO KNOBEL

Hoofdirekteur Nasionale Parkeraad 1953-1979
Chief Director National Parks Board 1953-1979
Directeur en Chef National Parks Board 1953-1979
Direktionsleiter National Parks Board 1953-1979

Struik Publishers
(an operating division of Struik Holdings (Pty) Ltd)
Struik House, Oswald Pirow Street
Foreshore, Cape Town 8001

Reg. No.: 80/02842/07

First published by the National Parks Board, Pretoria
Revised edition published by Struik Publishers 1988

Designed by Robert Meas
Edited by John Comrie-Greig
Translated into French by F. S. Helluy-Endenburg
Revised material translated into German by Rolf Annas
Illustrated by Hans Kumpf
Photoset by ProSet Laser Typesetting Bureau, Cape Town
Reproduction by Unifoto (Pty) Ltd, Cape Town
Reproduction of cover by Hirt & Carter (Pty) Ltd, Cape Town
Printed and bound by CTP Book Printers, Parow

ISBN 0 86977 702 5
BD8379

SOOGDIERE
VAN DIE KRUGERWILDTUIN EN ANDER NASIONALE PARKE

Saamgestel deur die Nasionale Parkeraad
Kunswerk: H. Kumpf

Uitgegee deur Struik Uitgewers in samewerking met die Nasionale Parkeraad

MAMMALS
OF THE KRUGER AND OTHER NATIONAL PARKS

Compiled by the National Parks Board
Artwork: H. Kumpf

Produced by Struik Publishers in collaboration with the National Parks Board

MAMMIFÈRES
DU PARC KRUGER ET DES AUTRES PARCS NATIONAUX

Établi par le National Parks Board
Artiste: H. Kumpf

Produit par Struik Publishers en collaboration avec le National Parks Board

SÄUGETIERE
IM KRUGER NATIONALPARK UND ANDEREN NATIONALPARKS

Zusammengestellt vom National Parks Board
Kunstdrucke: H. Kumpf

Herausgegeben von Struik Publishers gemeinsam mit dem National Parks Board

VOORWOORD

Soogdiere van die Krugerwildtuin en Ander Nasionale Parke was 'n opvolging van die *Suid-Afrikaanse Dieregids* en beleef nou sy dertiende hersiene en verbeterde uitgawe. Meer as 'n kwartmiljoen kopieë van die eerste twaalf uitgawes is verkoop en dit is dus baie duidelik dat die boekie aan sy doel beantwoord. Dit help die leser om meer van ons diere te wete te kom, om die een soort van die ander te kan onderskei en sodoende 'n besoek aan ons nasionale parke te veraangenaam. Hierdie nuwe uitgawe sluit ook Franse en Duitse teks in, sodat dit tot voordeel kan strek van die groeiende getal oorsese besoekers in ons land.

Die opstellers het gepoog om ons soogdier-fauna aan ons lesers en besoekers voor te stel. Ek glo hulle het uitmuntend daarin geslaag. Uit die natuur kan ons elke dag leer en die kennis so opgedoen, verryk ons gees en denke. Mag die boekie u help in dié opsig.

Graag wil ek die Nasionale Parkeraad se opregte dank uitspreek teenoor die persone wat bygedra het tot die sukses van hierdie publikasie. In besonder wil ek my dank uitspreek teenoor die kunstenaar, mnr H. Kumpf, vir sy uitstekende werk, veral omdat ek besef dat hy werklik sy bes probeer het om lewensgetroue afbeeldings van die diere te gee. Sy bydrae word hoog waardeer.

Nie al die soogdiere in ons nasionale parke is in die gidsboekie uitgebeeld nie, maar wel die algemeenste soorte. Dit behoort egter geen afbreuk te doen aan die belangrikheid van veral die kleiner diere wat nie in dié uitgawe verskyn nie, maar wat ek hoop u met net soveel genot sal waarneem as dié wat meer dikwels gesien word en meer opvallend is.

A.M. BRYNARD
Hoofdirekteur (1979-1987)

FOREWORD

Mammals of the Kruger and Other National Parks succeeded the *South African Animal Guide*, and is now experiencing its thirteenth revised and improved edition. Over a quarter of a million copies of the first 12 editions have been sold and it is therefore quite clear that the publication fulfils its purpose of assisting the reader to know more about our animals, of enabling him to distinguish one kind from another, and thus allows him to derive greater pleasure from a visit to our national parks. This new edition also incorporates French and German text for the benefit of the increasing numbers of overseas visitors to our country.

The compilers have tried to introduce our mammalian fauna to our readers and visitors. I am convinced that they have succeeded excellently. We can learn from nature every day and the knowledge thus gained enriches our mind and thoughts; may this publication help you in this respect.

I wish to convey the National Parks Board's sincere appreciation to the persons who contributed towards the success of this publication. In particular I would like to express my thanks to the artist, Mr. H. Kumpf, for his excellent work, especially as I realise the great task involved in obtaining such true representations of the animals. His contribution is much appreciated.

Not all the mammals in our national parks are illustrated in this guide book - only the more common species. This fact does not, however, detract from the importance of the smaller creatures which do not appear in this publication but which, I trust, you will observe with as much pleasure as those more noticeable and more frequently seen.

A. M. BRYNARD
Chief Director (1979-1987)

PRÉFACE

Mammals of the Kruger and Other National Parks a succédé au *South African Animal Guide* et a été revu et corrigé 13 fois. Les sept premières éditions ont été imprimées à 260 000 exemplaires et toutes les éditions sont maintenant épuisées. Il est donc clair que cette publication remplit son but, qui est d'aider le lecteur à mieux connaître nos splendides animaux, de lui permettre d'identifier les différentes espèces, lui donnant ainsi la possibilité de tirer un plus grand plaisir de ses visites dans nos parcs nationaux. Cette nouvelle édition comprend des textes en français et en allemand destinés au nombre croissant de visiteurs étrangers dans notre pays.

Les auteurs de ce livre ont essayé de présenter notre faune aux lecteurs et aux visiteurs. Je ne doute pas qu'ils y aient réussi. Nous pouvons apprendre de la nature tous les jours et cette connaissance enrichit nos esprits ainsi que notre façon de penser. Puisse cette publication vous aider à cet égard!

Au nom du National Parks Board je tiens à exprimer nos sincères remerciements aux personnes ayant contribué au succès de cette publication.

Je tiens à remercier tout particulièrement l'artiste M. H. Kumpf pour son excellent travail, d'autant plus que je sais combien grande a été sa tâche pour produire d'authentiques illustrations des animaux. Nous apprécions beaucoup sa contribution.

Nous n'avons pas fourni d'illustrations de tous les mammifères de nos parcs nationaux dans ce livre, - uniquement des plus communs. Ce fait ne doit pas vous détourner de l'importance des autres créatures. Elles ne sont pas présentes dans cette publication, mais je suis sûr que vous éprouverez autant de plaisir à les voir que les espèces plus connues.

A.M.BRYNARD
Directeur en Chef (1979-1987)

VORWORT

Mammals of the Kruger and Other National Parks folgte dem *South African Animal Guide*. Seine dreizehnte überprüfte und verbesserte Auflage wird jetzt herausgegeben. Von den ersten zwölf Auflagen wurden bereits mehr als eine Viertelmillion Exemplare verkauft. Daraus geht hervor, daß diese Veröffentlichung ihren Zweck erfüllt, dem Leser zu helfen, unsere schönen Tiere besser kennenzulernen und die verschiedenen Wildsorten zu unterscheiden. Auf diese Weise wird ihm ein Besuch unserer Nationalparks mehr Freude bereiten. Diese neue Auflage, die den französischen, englischen und afrikaansen Text einschließt, berücksichtigt die zunehmende Anzahl der Besucher unseres Landes aus Übersee.

Die Herausgeber dieses Buches haben versucht, unsere Leser und Besucher mit unserer Tierwelt bekanntzumachen. Ich bin davon überzeugt, daß sie dies mit großem Erfolg getan haben. Wir lernen jeden Tag von der Natur. Das Wissen, das wir so erwerben, bereichert unseren Geist und unsere Gedanken. Möge diese Veröffentlichung Ihnen auch in dieser Hinsicht helfen.

Besonderen Dank möchte ich dem Künstler, Herrn H. Kumpf, für seine ausgezeichnete Arbeit aussprechen. Ich bin mir dessen bewußt, welche große Aufgabe es war, so lebensgetreue Tierbilder zu schaffen. Sein Beitrag wird hoch geschätzt.

Nicht alle Säugetiere in unseren Nationalparks sind in diesem Handbuch abgebildet, nur die häufigeren Arten. Dies sagt aber nicht, daß die kleineren Tiere, die nicht in diesem Handbuch erwähnt sind, keine Bedeutung haben. Im Gegenteil. Ich nehme an, daß Sie diese mit genau so viel Freude beobachten werden wie jene, die wahrnehmbarer sind und häufiger gesehen werden.

A.M. BRYNARD
Direktionsleiter(1979-1987)

INDEKS/
INHOUD

INDEX/
CONTENTS

INDEX/ CONTENU

INHALTS-VERZEICHNIS

Die Kalahari-gemsbok Nasionale Park is veral bekend vir sy trekwildsoorte soos elande, gemsbokke, rooihartbeeste, blouwildebeeste en springbokke. Hierdie diere kan steeds vryelik tussen die Kalahari-gemsbok Nasionale Park en Botswana se Gemsbok Nasionale Park migreer, met groot tropvormings.

Troppe wild, soos hierdie gemsbokke, word dikwels opgemerk in die (gewoonlik droë) beddings van die Auob- en Nossobriviere in die Kalahari-gemsbok Nasionale Park.

The Kalahari Gemsbok National Park is known for its migratory wildlife species. Animals such as the eland, gemsbok, red hartebeest, blue wildebeest and springbok still migrate freely between the Park and Botswana's adjoining Gemsbok National Park in large herds.

Herds of antelope, such as these gemsbok, can often be seen along the (usually dry) beds of the Auob and Nossob rivers in the Kalahari Gemsbok National Park.

Le Parc National Kalahari Gemsbok est connu pour ses espèces sauvages migratrices. Des troupeaux d'animaux - élands, gemsboks, bubales rouges, gorgons bleus et springboks - se déplacent librement entre le parc et le Botswana.

On rencontre souvent des troupeaux d'antilopes, tels ces gemsboks, le long des bancs des rivières Auob et Nossob (généralement asséchées) dans le Parc National Kalahari Gemsbok.

Der Kalahari Gemsbok Nationalpark ist für sein Wechselwild bekannt. Tiere, wie zum Beispiel die Elens-, Gems- und Kuhantilopen, die Gnus und die Springböcke, wechseln immer noch frei zwischen dem Park und dem angrenzenden Botswana.

Antilopenherden wie diese Gemsantilopen sind oft in den (meist trockenen) Flußläufen des Auob und Nossob im Kalahari Gemsbok Nationalpark zu sehen.

Die verspreiding van soogdiere is op die volgende bladsye opgeteken vir 11 van Suid-Afrika se 15 nasionale parke. Hulle is: Nasionale Krugerwildtuin, Golden Gate-Hoogland Nasionale Park, Bergkwagga Nasionale Park, Addo-olifant Nasionale Park, Tsitsikammabos Nasionale Park, Tsitsikammaseekus Nasionale Park, Bontebok Nasionale Park, Karoo Nasionale Park, Augrabieswaterval Nasionale Park, Kalahari-gemsbok Nasionale Park, Langebaan Nasionale Park.

Mammal occurrence is recorded in the following pages for 11 out of South Africa's 15 national parks. These are: Kruger National Park, Golden Gate Highlands National Park, Mountain Zebra National Park, Addo Elephant National Park, Tsitsikamma Forest National Park, Tsitsikamma Coastal National Park, Bontebok National Park, Karoo National Park, Augrabies Falls National Park, Kalahari Gemsbok National Park, Langebaan National Park.

Dans les pages qui suivent, la présence des mammifères est indiquée dans les 11 parcs nationaux suivants (sur un total de 15 parcs): le Parc National Kruger, le Parc National Golden Gate Highlands, le Parc National du Zèbre de Montagne, le Parc National Addo des Éléphants, le Parc National de la Forêt de Tsitsikamma, le Parc National de la Côte de Tsitsikamma, le Parc National Bontebok, le Parc National du Karoo, le Parc National des Chutes d'Augrabies, le Parc National Kalahari Gemsbok, le Parc National de Langebaan.

Hinweise auf das Vorkommen der Säugetiere beziehen sich auf 11 der 15 südafrikanischen Nationalparks, und zwar auf die folgenden: Kruger Nationalpark, Golden Gate Nationalpark, Mountain Zebra Nationalpark, Addo Elephant Nationalpark, Tsitsikamma Forest Nationalpark, Tsitsikamma Coastal Nationalpark, Bontebok Nationalpark, Karoo Nationalpark, Augrabies Falls Nationalpark, Kalahari Gemsbok Nationalpark, Langebaan Nationalpark.

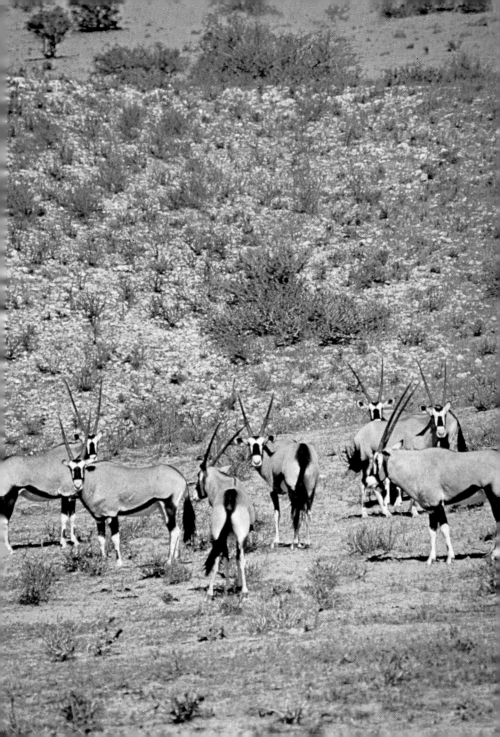

Groot troppe wild is geen seldsame gesig in die Nasionale Krugerwildtuin nie. Gemengde troppe met vier of meer groot soogdiersoorte vergader dikwels by watergate tussen 10h00 en 11h00.

In die Nasionale Krugerwildtuin kom daar in totaal 147 verskillende soogdiere voor, waarvan 51 soorte geklassifiseer word as 'groot' soogdiere en 96 as 'klein' soogdiere. Afgesien daarvan is daar reeds 507 verskillende voëlsoorte opgeteken asook 'n groot aantal reptiel-(114), amfibiese (33) en boomspesies (meer as 200).

Large herds of game are a frequent sight in the Kruger National Park. Mixed herds made up of four or more large mammal species often gather at water-holes between 10h00 and 11h00.

A total of 147 mammal species are to be found in the Kruger National Park, of which 51 are classified as 'large' mammals and 96 as 'small' mammals. In addition, 507 species of birds have been recorded in the Park, as well as a large number of reptile (114), amphibian (33) and tree species (over 200).

Il est fréquent de voir de larges troupeaux dans le Parc National Kruger. Des troupeaux de quatre espèces ou plus de larges mammifères se rassemblent généralement aux points d'eau entre 10h00 et 11h00.

Il y a en tout 147 espèces de mammifères dans le Parc National Kruger, dont 51 sont classées comme 'gros' mammifères et 96 comme 'petits' mammifères. En outre, on a dénombré 507 espèces d'oiseaux ainsi que de nombreux reptiles (114), amphibiens (33) et genres d'arbres (200).

Große Wildrudel sind oft im Kruger Nationalpark zu sehen. Rudel, die oft aus bis zu vier großen Wildarten bestehen, ziehen oft zwischen 10 und 11 Uhr zu den Wasserstellen.

Im Kruger Nationalpark kommen insgesamt 147 Säugetierarten vor. Von ihnen werden 51 als 'große' und 96 als 'kleine' Säugetiere klassifiziert. Außerdem wurden im Park neben 507 Vogelarten auch noch viele Reptilien (114), Amphibien (33) und Baumarten verzeichnet (200).

KRIMPVARKIE *Atelerix frontalis*

'n Nagdiertjie wat gewoonlik gedurende die dag in gate of onder beskutting skuil. Teen die aand kom hy uit om insekte, wurms, slakke, klein muise, akkedisse, eiers en selfs sagte vrugte vir kos te soek. As hy bedreig word, rol hy homself op in 'n stewige, stekelrige bal. Twee tot vier kleintjies word gedurende die somer gebore.

Massa . . . . .350 g
Lengte . . . . .15-20 cm
Draagtyd . . . . 35 dae

**KRUGER/GOLDEN GATE/
BERGKWAGGA**

HEDGEHOG *Atelerix frontalis*

Normally a nocturnal animal which hides in holes or under cover during the day. It is generally astir towards dusk to hunt for insects, worms, snails, small mice, lizards, eggs and also soft fruit. When threatened it rolls itself up into a tight spiny ball. Two to four young are born during summer.

Mass . . . . .350 g
Length . . . . .15-20 cm
Gestation period . . . . . . 35 days

**KRUGER/GOLDEN GATE/
MOUNTAIN ZEBRA**

LE HÉRISSON *Atelerix frontalis*

Généralement un animal nocturne qui se terre dans des trous ou reste à couvert pendant la journée. Il se déplace d'habitude au crépuscule à la recherche d'insectes, de vers, d'escargots, de souris, de lézards, d'oeufs, et aussi de fruits mous. Quand on le menace, il se met en boule. La femelle met bas de 2 à 4 petits en été.

Poids . . . . .350 g
Longueur . . . . .15-20 cm
Durée de la gestation . . . . . 35 jours

**KRUGER/GOLDEN GATE/
ZÈBRE DE MONTAGNE**

IGEL *Atelerix frontalis*

Der Igel ist normalerweise ein Nachttier, das sich während des Tages in Löchern oder anderen Schlupfwinkeln verbirgt. Er ist gewöhnlich in der Dämmerung unterwegs, um Insekten, Würmer, Schnecken, Mäuse und Eidechsen zu jagen. Auch Eier und weiche Früchte dienen ihm als Nahrung. Wenn er sich bedroht fühlt, rollt er sich zu einer festen, stacheligen Kugel zusammen. Zwei bis 4 Junge werden im Sommer geboren.

Gewicht . . . . .350 g
Länge . . . . .15-20 cm
Trächtigkeitszeit . . . . 35 Tage

**KRUGER/GOLDEN GATE/
MOUNTAIN ZEBRA**

BLOUAAP *Cercopithecus aethiops*

Dié diertjie het geen vaste paringseisoen nie. 'n Enkele kleintjie word gebore. Algemeen in bosagtige omgewings van die Nasionale Krugerwildtuin en Addo-olifant Nasionale Park en word dikwels in sommige van ons ander parke opgemerk.

Massa	5 kg
Lengte van liggaam	50 cm
Stertlengte	65 cm
Moontlike lewensduur	24 jaar
Draagtyd	7 maande

**KRUGER/BERGKWAGGA/
ADDO/TSITSIKAMMA/
KAROO/AUGRABIES**

VERVET MONKEY *Cercopithecus aethiops*

This animal has no fixed mating season. A single young is born. Common in the bushy regions of the Kruger and the Addo Elephant national parks and frequently seen in some of our other parks.

Mass	5 kg
Length of body	50 cm
Length of tail	65 cm
Potential longevity	24 years
Gestation period	7 months

**KRUGER/MOUNTAIN ZEBRA/
ADDO/TSITSIKAMMA/
KAROO/AUGRABIES**

LE GRIVET *Cercopithecus aethiops*

Cet animal n'a pas de saison de reproduction fixe. Il n'y a qu'un petit par portée. On le trouve surtout dans les régions arbustives du Parc National Kruger et du Parc National Addo des Éléphants, mais également dans certains autres parcs.

Poids	5 kg
Longueur du corps	50 cm
Longueur de la queue	65 cm
Longévité	24 ans
Durée de la gestation	7 mois

**KRUGER/ZÈBRE DE
MONTAGNE/ADDO/
TSITSIKAMMA/KAROO/
AUGRABIES**

BLAUAFFE *Cercopithecus aethiops*

Dieses Tier hat keine feste Paarungszeit. Nur ein Junges wird geboren. Es kommt häufig in den Buschgegenden des Kruger- und Addo Elephant Nationalparks vor und kann auch oft in einigen unserer anderen Parks gesehen werden.

Gewicht	5 kg
Körperlänge	50 cm
Schwanzlänge	65 cm
Mögliche Lebensdauer	24 Jahre
Trächtigkeitszeit	7 Monate

**KRUGER/MOUNTAIN
ZEBRA/ADDO/TSITSIKAMMA/
KAROO/AUGRABIES**

KAAPSE BOBBEJAAN *Papio ursinus*

Die bobbejaan kom algemeen in die Nasionale Krugerwildtuin voor, veral in die koppies om Pretoriuskop en langs al die rivieroewers. Dit is volwasse op die ouderdom van 8 jaar. Ou mannetjies het soms 'n liggaamsmassa van tot 45 kg. Daar is geen vaste paringseisoen nie. 'n Enkele kleintjie word gebore.

Massa (mannetjie)	. . . . .30 kg
Skouerhoogte	. . . . 75 cm
Stertlengte	. . . . 60 cm
Moontlike lewensduur	. . . . . 45 jaar
Draagtyd	. . . . 6 maande

KRUGER/GOLDEN GATE/ BERGKWAGGA/ TSITSIKAMMA/KAROO/ AUGRABIES/KALAHARI- GEMSBOK

CHACMA BABOON *Papio ursinus*

The baboon is common in the Kruger National Park particularly in the hills around Pretoriuskop and along all the rivers. At 8 years it is full-grown. Old males may have a body mass of up to 45 kg. It has no fixed mating season and single births are the rule.

Mass (male)	. . . . .30 kg
Shoulder height	. . . . 75 cm
Length of tail	. . . . 60 cm
Potential longevity	. . . . . 45 years
Gestation period	. . . . . .6 months

KRUGER/GOLDEN GATE/MOUN- TAIN ZEBRA/TSITSIKAMMA/ KAROO/AUGRABIES/ KALAHARI GEMSBOK

LE BABOUIN CHACMA *Papio ursinus*

Ce babouin est très répandu dans le Parc National Kruger, surtout dans les collines autour de Pretoriuskop et le long des rivières. Il atteint sa taille adulte à huit ans. Les vieux mâles peuvent peser jusqu'à 40 kg. Cet animal n'a pas de saison de reproduction fixe. La femelle ne met généralement bas qu'un seul petit.

Poids du mâle	. . . . .30 kg
Hauteur au garrot	. . . . 75 cm
Longueur de la queue	. . . . . 60 cm
Longévité	. . . . 45 ans
Durée de la gestation	. . . . . . 6 mois

KRUGER/GOLDEN GATE/ ZÈBRE DE MONTAGNE/ TSITSIKAMMA/KAROO/ AUGRABIES/KALAHARI GEMSBOK

PAVIAN *Papio ursinus*

Der Pavian kommt allgemein im Kruger Nationalpark, besonders in den Hügeln bei Pretoriuskop und an allen Flußläufen vor. Mit 8 Jahren ist er ausgewachsen. Alte Männchen können bis zu 45 kg wiegen. Das Tier hat keine bestimmte Paarungszeit, und in der Regel wird nur ein Junges geboren.

Gewicht (Männchen)	. . . . . .30 kg
Schulterhöhe	. . . . 75 cm
Schwanzlänge	. . . . 60 cm
Mögliche Lebensdauer	. . . . 45 Jahre
Trächtigkeitszeit	. . . . . . .6 Monate

KRUGER/GOLDEN GATE/MOUN- TAIN ZEBRA/TSITSIKAMMA/ KAROO/AUGRABIES/ KALAHARI GEMSBOK

IETERMAGOG *Manis temminckii*

Die liggaam, behalwe aan die onderkant, is met harde horingskubbe oortrek. Die ietermagog is hoofsaaklik naglewend en woon in gate. Dit vreet miere en rysmiere deur die neste met goed ontwikkelde kloue oop te breek. As een aangeval word, rol hy hom in 'n bal op. 'n Enkele kleintjie word op 'n keer gebore.

Massa . . . . 8 kg
Lengte (met stert) . . . . 100 cm

KRUGER/KALAHARI-GEMSBOK

PANGOLIN *Manis temminckii*

The body, except for the underparts, is covered with hard, horny scales. The pangolin is mainly nocturnal and lives in a burrow. It feeds on ants and termites, breaking up the nests with its well-developed claws. When it is attacked it rolls itself into a tight ball. A single young is born.

Mass . . . . 8 kg
Length (with tail) . . . . 100 cm

KRUGER/KALAHARI GEMSBOK

LE PANGOLIN *Manis temminckii*

A l'exception des surfaces intérieures, le corps est recouvert d'écailles cornées et dures. Le pangolin a une activité principalement nocturne; il vit dans un terrier. C'est un mangeur de fourmis, dont il détruit les nids avec ses griffes extrêmement puissantes. En cas d'attaque, il s'enroule solidement. La femelle met bas un seul jeune.

Poids . . . . 8 kg
Longueur (avec la queue) . . . 100 cm

KRUGER/KALAHARI GEMSBOK

STEPPENSCHUPPENTIER *Manis temminckii*

Der Körper, mit Ausnahme des Unterleibes, ist mit harten, hornigen Schuppen bedeckt. Das Steppenschuppentier geht hauptsächlich nachts auf Nahrungssuche und lebt während des Tages in einem Bau. Es ernährt sich von Ameisen und Termiten, die es mit seinen gut entwickelten Klauen aufgräbt. Wenn es angegriffen wird, rollt es sich zu einem festen Ball zusammen. Ein einziges Junges wird geboren.

Gewicht . . . . 8 kg
Länge (mit Schwanz) . . . . . 100 cm

KRUGER/KALAHARI GEMSBOK

LEEU *Panthera leo*

Paring vind plaas dwarsdeur die jaar maar bereik 'n hoogtepunt in die herfs of vroeë winter; 2-5 kleintjies word per werpsel gebore. Die leeubevolking van die Tshokwane-gebied van die Nasionale Krugerwildtuin lewer nou en dan 'n sogenaamde 'witleeu' op. Dit word veroorsaak deur 'n seldsame genetiese toestand wat aan albinisme verwant is, maar verskil in die opsig dat daar wel donker pigment teenwoordig is.

Massa (mannetjie)	200 kg
Skouerhoogte (mannetjie)	125 cm
Loopsnelheid	4 km/h
Stormsnelheid	60 km/h
Moontlike lewensduur	20 jaar
Draagtyd	3,5 maande

KRUGER/KALAHARI-GEMSBOK

LION *Panthera leo*

Mating takes place throughout the year but peaks in autumn or early winter; 2 to 5 cubs are born per litter. The lion population of the Tshokwane area of the Kruger National Park occasionally produces a so-called 'white' lion. This is caused by a rare genetic condition related to albinism but differing in that some dark pigment is present.

Mass (male)	200 kg
Shoulder height (male)	125 cm
Walking speed	4 km/h
Charging speed	60 km/h
Potential longevity	20 years
Gestation period	3,5 months

KRUGER/KALAHARI GEMSBOK

LE LION *Panthera leo*

L'accouplement prend place toute l'année, mais surtout en automne ou au début de l'hiver. La femelle met bas de 2 à 5 lionceaux. On rencontre parfois dans la région de Tshokwane (Parc National Kruger) un lion 'blanc'. C'est un phénomène d'origine génétique, apparenté à l'albinisme. Il s'en distingue cependant par la présence de quelques pigments foncés.

Poids du mâle	200 kg
Hauteur au garrot (mâle)	125 cm
Vitesse de marche	4 km/h
Vitesse de charge	60 km/h
Longévité	20 ans
Durée de la gestation	3 mois

KRUGER/KALAHARI GEMSBOK

LÖWE *Panthera leo*

Die Paarung findet das ganze Jahr über statt, meist jedoch im Herbst oder Frühwinter. Es werden 2 bis 5 Junge pro Wurf geboren. Im Tshokwane-Gebiet des Kruger Nationalparks wird ab und zu ein sogenannter 'weißer' Löwe geboren. Diese Erscheinung wird durch einen seltenen genetischen Zustand, der dem Albinismus verwandt ist, verursacht. Der Unterschied besteht darin, daß ein wenig dunkles Pigment vorkommt.

Gewicht (Männchen)	200 kg
Schulterhöhe (Männchen)	125 cm
Schrittschnelligkeit	4 km/h
Angriffsschnelligkeit	60 km/h
Mögliche Lebensdauer	20 Jahre
Trächtigkeitszeit	3,5 Monate

KRUGER/KALAHARI GEMSBOK

LUIPERD *Panthera pardus*

'n Nagdier wat algemeen in die Nasionale Krugerwildtuin en Kalahari-gemsbok Nasionale Park voorkom. Dit verskil van die jagluiperd deurdat sy kolle onderbroke en rosetvormig is. Die liggaamsbou is kort, stewig en katagtig, die kop massief en die toonnaels kan heeltemal teruggetrek word. Twee tot 3 kleintjies word per werpsel gebore.

Massa (mannetjie)	60 kg
Skouerhoogte (mannetjie)	60 cm
Moontlike lewensduur	21 jaar
Draagtyd	3 maande

**KRUGER/TSITSIKAMMA/
KAROO/AUGRABIES/
KALAHARI-GEMSBOK**

LEOPARD *Panthera pardus*

A nocturnal animal common in the Kruger and the Kalahari Gemsbok national parks. It differs from the cheetah in that its spots are arranged in rosettes. The body is compactly built and cat-like, the head massive, and the claws fully retractile. Two to 3 young are born per litter.

Mass (male)	60 kg
Shoulder height (male)	60 cm
Potential longevity	21 years
Gestation period	3 months

**KRUGER/TSITSIKAMMA/
KAROO/AUGRABIES/
KALAHARI GEMSBOK**

LE LÉOPARD *Panthera pardus*

C'est un animal nocturne commun dans les parcs nationaux Kruger et Kalahari Gemsbok. Il se distingue du guépard par ses taches qui sont en forme de rosettes. Le corps est compact et bâti comme celui du chat. La tête est massive et les griffes totalement rétractiles. La femelle donne naissance à 2 ou 3 petits.

Poids du mâle	60 kg
Hauteur au garrot (mâle)	60 cm
Longévité	21 ans
Durée de la gestation	3 mois

**KRUGER/TSITSIKAMMA/
KAROO/AUGRABIES/
KALAHARI GEMSBOK**

LEOPARD *Panthera pardus*

Der Leopard ist ein Nachttier, das allgemein im Kruger- und Kalahari Gemsbok Nationalpark vorkommt. Er unterscheidet sich vom Geparden dadurch, daß seine Flecken rosettenförmig angeordnet sind. Der Körper ist stark gebaut und ähnelt dem einer Katze. Der Kopf ist massiv, und die Klauen können vollkommen zurückgezogen werden. Es werden 2 bis 3 Junge pro Wurf geboren.

Gewicht (Männchen)	60 kg
Schulterhöhe (Männchen)	60 cm
Mögliche Lebensdauer	21 Jahre
Trächtigkeitszeit	3 Monate

**KRUGER/TSITSIKAMMA/
KAROO/AUGRABIES/
KALAHARI GEMSBOK**

JAGLUIPERD *Acinonyx jubatus*

Verskil van die luiperd daarin dat die kolle solied, ovaal en rond is. Die liggaam is slank en gebou vir spoed. Die kop is klein met 'n duidelike swart streep wat van elke oog tot in die mondhoeke strek. Die toonnaels kan net gedeeltelik teruggetrek word. Van 2 tot 4 kleintjies word per werpsel gebore.

Massa	.50 kg
Skouerhoogte	. 75 cm
Moontlike lewensduur	. 15 jaar
Draagtyd	. 3 maande
Vinnigste spoed	.100 km/h

KRUGER/KALAHARI-GEMSBOK

CHEETAH *Acinonyx jubatus*

The cheetah differs from the leopard in that it is marked with 'solid' oval and round spots. The body is slender and built for speed. The head is small with two conspicuous black lines running from the eyes to the corners of the mouth. The claws are semi-retractile. From 2 to 4 young are born per litter.

Mass	.50 kg
Shoulder height	. 75 cm
Potential longevity	. 15 years
Gestation period	.3 months
Fastest speed	. 100 km/h

KRUGER/KALAHARI GEMSBOK

LE GUÉPARD *Acinonyx jubatus*

Le guépard se distingue du léopard par ses taches nettement marquées et de forme ovale ou ronde. Le corps est élancé et bâti pour la course. La tête est petite avec deux lignes noires bien visibles allant des yeux aux coins de la gueule. Les griffes sont semi-rétractiles. La femelle met bas de 2 à 4 petits.

Poids	.50 kg
Hauteur au garrot	. 75 cm
Longévité	. 15 ans
Durée de la gestation	. 3 mois
Record de vitesse	.100 km/h

KRUGER/KALAHARI GEMSBOK

GEPARD *Acinonyx jubatus*

Der Gepard unterscheidet sich vom Leoparden dadurch, daß seine dunklen Flecken rund oder oval sind. Der Körper ist schlank und für Schnelligkeit gebaut. Der Kopf ist schmal. Er hat zwei auffallende Linien, die von den Augen zu den Maulwinkeln laufen. Die Klauen können teilweise zurückgezogen werden. Zwei bis 4 Junge werden pro Wurf geboren.

Gewicht	.50 kg
Schulterhöhe	. 75 cm
Mögliche Lebensdauer	. 15 Jahre
Trächtigkeitszeit	.3 Monate
Die größte Schnelligkeit	. .100 km/h

KRUGER/KALAHARI GEMSBOK

TIERBOSKAT *Felis serval*

'n Langbenige kat met 'n klein koppie en groot ore, en met aantreklike kolle op 'n geelbruin agtergrond. Op die rug verander die kolle in strepe. Die stert is kort. Dit vang hoofsaaklik klein soogdiertjies en voëls vir kos maar vreet ook dikwels insekte, o.a. kewers. Daar is 1-5 (gewoonlik 3) kleintjies per werpsel.

Massa	. . . . .10 kg
Skouerhoogte	. . . . 60 cm
Lengte (met stert)	. . . . . . .115 cm
Draagtyd	. . . . 70 dae

KRUGER

SERVAL *Felis serval*

A long-legged cat with a small head and large ears, handsomely marked with dark spots on a tawny background. On the back the spots become elongated to form stripes. The tail is short. It feeds chiefly on small mammals and birds but also eats insects, especially beetles. Its litters consist of 1 to 5 (usually 3) kittens.

Mass	. . . . .10 kg
Shoulder height	. . . . 60 cm
Length (with tail)	. . . . . . .115 cm
Gestation period	. . . . 70 days

KRUGER

LE SERVAL *Felis serval*

Un félin aux longues pattes, à la tête petite, aux larges oreilles et à la belle robe brune tachetée de noir. Sur le dos les taches s'allongent pour former des rayures. La queue est courte. Il se nourrit surtout de petits mammifères et d'oiseaux, mais également d'insectes et particulièrement de coléoptères. La femelle met bas de 1 à 5 petits (générale-ment 3).

Poids	. . . . .10 kg
Hauteur	. . . . 60 cm
Longueur (avec la queue)	. . .115 cm
Durée de la gestation	. . . . . 70 jours

KRUGER

BUSCHKATZE oder SERVAL *Felis serval*

Eine langbeinige Katze mit schmalem Kopf und großen Ohren. Sie ist hübsch gezeichnet mit dunklen Flecken auf einem lohfarbenen Hintergrund. Am Rücken sind die Flecken langgezogen, daß sie Streifen bilden. Der Schwanz ist kurz. Ihre Nahrung besteht hauptsächlich aus kleinen Säugetieren und Vögeln. Sie frißt aber auch Insekten, besonders Käfer. Ein Wurf besteht aus 1 bis 5 (meistens 3) Jungen.

Gewicht	. . . . .10 kg
Schulterhöhe	. . . . 60 cm
Länge (mit Schwanz)	. . . . . .115 cm
Trächtigkeitszeit	. . . . 70 Tage

KRUGER

ROOIKAT *Felis caracal*

Hierdie mediumgroot kat word in die meeste van ons nasionale parke aangetref. Die kleur is geelrooi en die gepunte ore dra elk 'n klossie swart hare aan die punte. Vang voëls en klein soogdiertjies nie groter as klein antilope. Van 2 tot 3 kleintjies word per werpsel gebore.

Massa . . . . .13 kg
Skouerhoogte . . . . 40 cm
Lengte (met stert) . . . . 85 cm

**KRUGER/GOLDEN GATE/
BERGKWAGGA/ADDO/
KALAHARI-GEMSBOK/
LANGEBAAN**

CARACAL *Felis caracal*

This medium-sized cat is found in most of our national parks. It is yellowish-red in colour and the pointed ears bear tufts of black hair at the ends. Preys on birds and small mammals up to the size of small antelope. Two to 3 young are born per litter.

Mass . . . . .13 kg
Shoulder height . . . . 40 cm
Length (with tail) . . . . 85 cm

**KRUGER/GOLDEN GATE/MOUN-
TAINZEBRA/ADDO/KALAHARI
GEMSBOK/LANGEBAAN**

LE CARACAL *Felis caracal*

Ce félin de taille moyenne est présent dans la plupart des parcs nationaux. Il est de couleur jaune rouge et ses oreilles pointues se terminent par une sorte d'aigrette de poils noirs. Il se nourrit d'oiseaux et de petits mammifères dont la taille va jusqu'à de petites antilopes.

Poids . . . . .13 kg
Hauteur au garrot . . . . 40 cm
Longueur (avec la queue) . . . 85 cm

**KRUGER/GOLDEN
GATE/ZÈBRE DE MON-
TAGNE/ADDO/KALAHARI
GEMSBOK/LANGEBAAN**

KARAKAL oder WÜSTENLUCHS *Felis caracal*

Diese Katze mittlerer Größe wird in den meisten Nationalparks angetroffen. Ihre Färbung ist gelblich rot. Die Ohren haben schwarze Haarbüschel an den Spitzen. Dieses Tier erbeutet Vögel und kleinere Säugetiere bis zur Größe von kleinen Antilopen. Zwei bis 3 Junge werden pro Wurf geboren.

Gewicht . . . . .13 kg
Schulterhöhe . . . . 40 cm
Länge (mit Schwanz) . . . . . . 85 cm

**KRUGER/GOLDEN GATE/MOUN-
TAINZEBRA/ADDO/KALAHARI
GEMSBOK/LANGEBAAN**

MAANHAARJAKKALS *Proteles cristatus*

Die dier leef hoofsaaklik van rysmiere, maar vreet ook ander insekte. Omdat dit lomp en stadig is, word dit dikwels deur roofdiere gevang. Soms word dit van veediewery beskuldig, maar die dier se tande is te swak ontwikkel om vleis te vreet. Twee tot 4 kleintjies word per werpsel gebore.

Massa	9 kg
Hoogte	50 cm
Lengte (met stert)	90 cm
Draagtyd	2 maande

KRUGER/GOLDEN GATE/ BERGKWAGGA/BONTEBOK/ KAROO/AUGRABIES/ KALAHARI-GEMSBOK

AARDWOLF *Proteles cristatus*

This animal feeds mostly on termites, but also catches other insects. Owing to its clumsy and slow movements it is often caught by predators. It is sometimes accused of stock-killing, but its teeth are too poorly developed to deal with flesh. Two to 4 cubs are born per litter.

Mass	9 kg
Shoulder height	50 cm
Length (with tail)	90 cm
Gestation period	2 months

KRUGER/GOLDEN GATE/MOUN-TAIN ZEBRA/BONTEBOK/ KAROO/AUGRABIES/ KALAHARI GEMSBOK

LE PROTÈLE *Proteles cristatus*

Cet animal se nourrit surtout de termites, mais il chasse aussi d'autres insectes. A cause de ses mouvements gauches et lents il est souvent capturé par les prédateurs. On l'accuse parfois de tuer du bétail, mais sa denture n'est pas suffisamment développée pour lui permettre de s'attaquer à la chair. La femelle met bas de 2 à 4 petits.

Poids	9 kg
Hauteur	50 cm
Longueur (avec la queue)	90 cm
Durée de la gestation	2 mois

KRUGER/GOLDEN GATE/ ZÈBRE DE MONTAGNE/ BONTEBOK/KAROO/ AUGRABIES/ KALAHARI GEMSBOK

ERDWOLF *Proteles cristatus*

Der Erdwolf ernährt sich meist von Termiten, fängt aber auch andere Insekten. Da er sich schwerfällig und langsam bewegt, wird er oft von Raubtieren gefangen. Manchmal wird er davon beschuldigt, daß er Vieh reißt, aber seine Zähne sind zum Fleischfressen nicht gut genug entwickelt. Es werden 2 bis 4 Junge pro Wurf geboren.

Gewicht	9 kg
Schulterhöhe	50 cm
Länge (mit Schwanz)	90 cm
Trächtigkeitszeit	2 Monate

KRUGER/GOLDEN GATE/MOUN-TAIN ZEBRA/BONTEBOK/ KAROO/AUGRABIES/ KALAHARI GEMSBOK

GEVLEKTE HIËNA *Crocuta crocuta*

Die gevlekte hiëna is die grootste van die twee hiënaspesies en, hoewel hoofsaaklik naglewend, word dit dikwels gedurende die dag gesien. Dit is nie tweeslagtig soos so dikwels geglo word nie, en is ook nie 'n lafhartige aasvreter nie. Dit vreet wel aas maar is ook 'n aktiewe jagter. Gewoonlik word 2 tot 3 kleintjies per werpsel gebore.

Massa	.60 kg
Skouerhoogte	80 cm
Loopsnelheid	15 km/h
Hardloopsnelheid	45 km/h
Moontlike lewensduur	25 jaar
Draagtyd	3,5 maande

KRUGER/KALAHARI-GEMSBOK

SPOTTED HYAENA *Crocuta crocuta*

This is the larger of the two hyaena species and although mainly nocturnal it is commonly seen during the day. It is not hermaphroditic as is so commonly believed, nor is it a cowardly scavenger. It hunts actively as well as eating carrion. Usually 2 to 3 young are born per litter.

Mass	.60 kg
Shoulder height	80 cm
Walking speed	15 km/h
Running speed	45 km/h
Potential longevity	25 years
Gestation period	.3,5 months

KRUGER/KALAHARI GEMSBOK

L'HYÈNE TACHETÉE *Crocuta crocuta*

C'est la plus grande des deux espèces d'hyène et, bien qu'elle soit principalement nocturne, il est fréquent de la voir pendant la journée. En dépit de certaines croyances populaires, elle n'est pas hermaphrodite. Ce n'est pas non plus simplement un lâche charognard car elle chasse elle-même. La femelle donne généralement le jour à 2 ou 3 petits.

Poids	.60 kg
Hauteur au garrot	80 cm
Vitesse de marche	15 km/h
Vitesse de course	45 km/h
Longévité	25 ans
Durée de la gestation	3,5 mois

KRUGER/KALAHARI GEMSBOK

GEFLECKTE HYÄNE *Crocuta crocuta*

Die gefleckte Hyäne ist die größere der beiden Hyänenarten. Obgleich sie als Nachttier bezeichnet wird, ist sie auch häufig tagsüber zu sehen. Sie ist kein Zwitter, wie oft vermutet wird, und auch kein feiger Aasfresser. Sie lebt sowohl von der Jagd als auch von Aas. Gewöhnlich werden 2 bis 3 Junge geboren.

Gewicht	.60 kg
Schulterhöhe	80 cm
Schrittschnelligkeit	15 km/h
Laufschnelligkeit	45 km/h
Mögliche Lebensdauer	25 Jahre
Trächtigkeitszeit	3,5 Monate

KRUGER/KALAHARI GEMSBOK

STRANDJUT *Hyaena brunnea*

Dit is 'n aasvretende nagdier en word dikwels deur leeus en gevlekte hiënas doodgemaak as hulle te naby die prooi kom. Van 2 tot 4 kleintjies word gebore.

Massa	.40 kg
Skouerhoogte	80 cm
Moontlike lewensduur	24 jaar
Draagtyd	3 maande

KRUGER/KALAHARI-GEMSBOK

BROWN HYAENA *Hyaena brunnea*

It is a nocturnal scavenger and is sometimes killed by lions and spotted hyaenas at kills if it becomes too venturesome. From 2 to 4 young are born.

Mass	.40 kg
Shoulder height	80 cm
Potential longevity	24 years
Gestation period	.3 months

KRUGER/KALAHARI GEMSBOK

L'HYÈNE BRUNE *Hyaena brunnea*

C'est un charognard nocturne parfois tué par les lions et les hyènes tachetées si elle s'approche trop des proies. Elle a de 2 à 4 petits par portée.

Poids	.40 kg
Hauteur au garrot	80 cm
Longévité	24 ans
Durée de la gestation	3 mois

KRUGER/KALAHARI GEMSBOK

SCHABRACKENHYÄNE *Hyaena brunnea*

Sie ist ein nächtlicher Aasfresser und wird manchmal an einem Riß von Löwen oder gefleckten Hyänen getötet, wenn sie zu waghalsig wird. Zwei bis 4 Junge werden geboren.

Gewicht	.40 kg
Schulterhöhe	80 cm
Mögliche Lebensdauer	24 Jahre
Trächtigkeitszeit	.3 Monate

KRUGER/KALAHARI GEMSBOK

BAKOORJAKKALS   *Otocyon megalotis*

'n Klein skadelose diertjie wat van insekte, muise en wilde vrugte leef. Gewoonlik word van 3 tot 5 kleintjies per werpsel gebore. Dit hou van droër streke, maar het onlangs sy verspreidingsgebied uitgebrei en is in 1967 vir die eerste keer in die Nasionale Krugerwildtuin opgeteken.

Massa . . . . 4 kg
Skouerhoogte . . . . 30 cm
Lengte (met stert) . . . . 80 cm
Draagtyd . . . . 2 maande

**KRUGER/BERGKWAGGA/
ADDO/KAROO/AUGRABIES/
KALAHARI-GEMSBOK/
LANGEBAAN**

BAT-EARED FOX   *Otocyon megalotis*

This fox is also known as Delalande's fox. A small harmless animal which feeds on insects, mice and wild fruit. Usually 3 to 5 young are born per litter. It prefers more arid country but has recently expanded its range and was recorded for the first time in the Kruger National Park in 1967.

Mass . . . . 4 kg
Shoulder height . . . . 30 cm
Length (with tail) . . . . 80 cm
Gestation period . . . . . . .2 months

**KRUGER/MOUNTAIN
ZEBRA/ADDO/KAROO/
AUGRABIES/KALAHARI
GEMSBOK/LANGEBAAN**

L'OTOCYON   *Otocyon megalotis*

Ce parent du chacal est aussi connu sous le nom de renard de Delalande. C'est un petit animal inoffensif qui se nourrit d'insectes, de souris et de fruits sauvages. On compte généralement 3 à 5 petits par portée. Il a pour habitat les zones arides mais a récemment commencé à peupler d'autres régions. On a noté sa présence dans le Parc National Kruger pour la première fois en 1967.

Poids . . . . 4 kg
Hauteur au garrot . . . . 80 cm
Longueur (avec la queue) . . . 30 cm
Durée de la gestation . . . . . 2 mois

**KRUGER/ZÈBRE DE MON-
TAGNE/ADDO/KAROO/
AUGRABIES/KALAHARI
GEMSBOK/LANGEBAAN**

LÖFFELHUND   *Otocyon megalotis*

Der Löffelhund, auch unter dem Namen Delalandes Fuchs bekannt, ist ein kleines harmloses Tier, das von Insekten, Mäusen und wilden Früchten lebt. Gewöhnlich werden 3 bis 5 Junge geboren. Das Tier bevorzugt trockene Gegenden, aber ist seit einiger Zeit weiter verbreitet und wurde 1967 zum ersten Mal im Kruger Nationalpark verzeichnet.

Gewicht . . . . 4 kg
Schulterhöhe . . . . 30 cm
Länge (mit Schwanz) . . . . . 80 cm
Trächtigkeitszeit . . . . . . .2 Monate

**KRUGER/MOUNTAIN
ZEBRA/ADDO/KAROO/
AUGRABIES/KALAHARI
GEMSBOK/LANGEBAAN**

SILWERVOS *Vulpes chama*

Die silwervos is 'n nagdiertjie wat hoofsaaklik leef van
insekte, muise, hase en voëls wat op die grond slaap, maar
dit is ook 'n aasvreter en sal vrugte vreet. Drie tot 4
kleintjies word per werpsel gebore.

Massa . . . . 3 kg
Skouerhoogte . . . . 30 cm
Draagtyd . . . . 52 dae

**GOLDEN GATE/BERGKWAGGA/
ADDO/BONTEBOK/
KAROO/KALAHARI
GEMSBOK/LANGEBAAN**

CAPE FOX *Vulpes chama*

The Cape fox or silver jackal is a nocturnal animal. Feeds
mainly on insects, mice, hares and ground-roosting birds,
but it is also a scavenger and will take wild fruit. Three or 4
young are born per litter.

Mass . . . . 3 kg
Shoulder height . . . . 30 cm
Gestation period . . . . . . 52 days

**GOLDEN GATE/MOUNTAIN
ZEBRA/ADDO/BONTEBOK/
KAROO/KALAHARI
GEMSBOK/LANGEBAAN**

LE RENARD DU CAP *Vulpes chama*

Le renard du Cap (ou chacal argenté) est un animal
nocturne. Il se nourrit principalement d'insectes, de souris,
de lièvres et d'oiseaux qui nichent sur terre, mais également
de charognes et de fruits sauvages. La femelle donne le
jour à 3 ou 4 jeunes.

Poids . . . . 3 kg
Hauteur au garrot . . . . 30 cm
Durée de la gestation . . . . . 52 jours

**GOLDEN GATE/ZÈBRE DE MON-
TAGNE/ADDO/BONTEBOK/
KAROO/KALAHARI
GEMSBOK/LANGEBAAN**

SILBERRÜCKENFUCHS oder KAMA *Vulpes chama*

Der Silberrückenfuchs oder Kama ist ein Nachttier, das sich
meist von Insekten, Mäusen, Hasen und Vögeln, die auf der
Erde brüten, ernährt. Auch Aas und wilde Früchte dienen
ihm als Nahrung. In einem Wurf werden 3 oder 4 Junge
geboren.

Gewicht . . . . 3 kg
Schulterhöhe . . . . 30 cm
Trächtigkeitszeit . . . . . . 52 Tage

**GOLDEN GATE/MOUNTAIN
ZEBRA/ADDO/BONTEBOK/
KAROO/KALAHARI
GEMSBOK/LANGEBAAN**

ROOIJAKKALS *Canis mesomelas*

Dit is 'n aasvreter wat ook klein soogdiertjies en voëls vang. Word gekenmerk deur die swart 'saal' met 'n sprinkeling van wit hare oor die rug. Een tot 6 kleintjies word per werpsel gebore.

Massa (mannetjie)	8 kg
Skouerhoogte	40 cm
Moontlike lewensduur	10 jaar
Draagtyd	2 maande

ALMAL BEHALWE TSITSIKAMMA

BLACK-BACKED JACKAL *Canis mesomelas*

It is a scavenger, but also preys on small mammals and birds. The black 'saddle' on the back with its sprinkling of white hairs is a characteristic of this animal. From 1 to 6 (usually 3) young are born per litter.

Mass (male)	8 kg
Shoulder height	40 cm
Potential longevity	10 years
Gestation period	2 months

ALL NATIONAL PARKS EXCEPT TSITSIKAMMA

LE CHACAL AU DOS NOIR *Canis mesomelas*

C'est un charognard mais il s'attaque aussi à de petits mammifères et à des oiseaux. Cet animal se distingue par une 'selle' noire parsemée de poils blancs sur le dos. La femelle met bas de 1 à 6 jeunes (généralement 3).

Poids du mâle	8 kg
Hauteur au garrot	40 cm
Longévité	10 ans
Durée de la gestation	2 mois

DANS TOUS LES PARCS NATIONAUX A L'EXCEPTION DE CEUX DE TSITSIKAMMA

SCHABRACKENSCHAKAL *Canis mesomelas*

Der Schabrackenschakal ist ein Aasfresser, aber er fängt auch kleine Säugetiere und Vögel. Der schwarze 'Sattel' am Rücken mit den vereinzelten weißen Haaren, ist ein charakteristisches Zeichen für das Tier. Eins bis 6 Junge werden pro Wurf geboren.

Gewicht (Männchen)	8 kg
Schulterhöhe	40 cm
Mögliche Lebensdauer	10 Jahre
Trächtigkeitszeit	2 Monate

IN ALLEN NATIONALPARKS AUSSER IM TSITSIKAMMA NATIONALPARK

WITKWASJAKKALS *Canis adustus*

'n Sku en seldsame spesies wat in die Nasionale Krugerwildtuin aangetref word. Hulle leef van klein soogdiertjies, eiers, insekte, voëls wat op die grond slaap asook vrugte. Van 4 tot 6 kleintjies word per werpsel gebore. Gekenmerk deur 'n algemene grys kleur en die duidelike ligte en donker streep op elke blad; die punt van die stert is gewoonlik wit.

Massa	9 kg
Skouerhoogte	38 cm
Draagtyd	2 maande

KRUGER

SIDE-STRIPED JACKAL *Canis adustus*

A timid and rare species found in the Kruger National Park. Feeds on small mammals, ground-roosting birds, eggs, insects and wild fruit. From 4 to 6 young are born per litter. Characterized by overall greyish colour and by the clear light-and-dark stripe along each flank; the tip of the tail is usually white.

Mass	9 kg
Shoulder height	38 cm
Gestation period	2 months

KRUGER

LE CHACAL A RAYURES LATÉRALES *Canis adustus*

C'est une espèce de chacal timide et rare que l'on trouve dans le Parc National Kruger. Il se nourrit de petits mammifères, d'oiseaux qui nichent sur terre, d'oeufs, d'insectes et parfois de fruits. Cet animal est caractérisé par un pelage grisâtre et une nette rayure sombre et claire le long de chaque flanc. Le bout de la queue est générale-ment blanc. La femelle donne le jour à entre 4 et 6 jeunes.

Poids	9 kg
Hauteur au garrot	38 cm
Durée de la gestation	2 mois

KRUGER

STREIFENSCHAKAL *Canis adustus*

Ein furchtsames und seltenes Tier, das im Kruger Nationalpark vorkommt. Es ernährt sich von kleinen Säugetieren, Vögeln, die auf der Erde brüten, Eiern, Insekten und wilden Früchten. Vier bis 6 Junge werden pro Wurf geboren. Charakteristisch ist das gräuliche Fell mit den deutlichen hell-und-dunklen Streifen an jeder Flanke. Die Schwanzspitze ist meistens weiß.

Gewicht	9 kg
Schulterhöhe	38 cm
Trächtigkeitszeit	2 Monate

KRUGER

WILDEHOND *Lycaon pictus*

Wildehonde jag gewoonlik in troppe. Die prooi word gejaag en in die hardloop verskeur, totdat dit ineensak van skok en bloedverlies. Gewoonlik word tussen 7 en 10 kleintjies gedurende die winter gebore.

Massa	.25 kg
Skouerhoogte (mannetjie)	. . . 75 cm
Volgehoue jagspoed	. . . . . 66 km/h
Moontlike lewensduur	. . . . . 10 jaar
Draagtyd	. . . . 70 dae

KRUGER/
KALAHARI-GEMSBOK

HUNTING DOG *Lycaon pictus*

Hunting dogs usually hunt in packs, and the prey is generally mauled while fleeing until it collapses from shock and loss of blood. Usually between 7 and 10 young are born during the winter.

Mass	. . . . 25 kg
Shoulder height (male)	. . . . . 75 cm
Sustainable pursuit speed	. . 66 km/h
Potential longevity	. . . . . . 10 years
Gestation period	. . . . 70 days

KRUGER/
KALAHARI GEMSBOK

LE LYCAON *Lycaon pictus*

Les lycaons chassent habituellement en meute et lacèrent la proie pendant qu'elle cherche à fuir, jusqu'à ce qu'elle tombe, terrifiée et exsangue. La femelle met généralement bas de 6 à 10 petits pendant l'hiver.

Poids	. . . . .25 kg
Hauteur au garrot (mâle)	. . . . 75 cm
Vitesse de chasse	. . . . . . 66 km/h
Longévité	. . . . 10 ans
Durée de la gestation	. . . . . 70 jours

KRUGER/
KALAHARI GEMSBOK

HYÄNENHUND *Lycaon pictus*

Der Hyänenhund jagt meistens in Rudeln und zerreißt die Beute auf der Flucht, bis sie wegen Schock und Blutverlust zusammenbricht. Meistens werden 7 bis 10 Junge im Winter geboren.

Gewicht	. . . . .25 kg
Schulterhöhe (Männchen)	. . . 75 cm
Dauerschnelligkeit	. . . . . . 66 km/h
Mögliche Lebensdauer	. . . . 10 Jahre
Trächtigkeitszeit	. . . . 70 Tage

KRUGER/
KALAHARI GEMSBOK

STINKMUISHOND *Ictonyx striatus*

Die stinkmuishond is hoofsaaklik 'n nagdier. Twee tot 3
kleintjies word gewoonlik per werpsel gebore. Bekend
vanweë die onwelriekende vloeistof wat dit uit die anale
kliere spuit om vyande mee af te weer. Dit voed op insekte,
knaagdiere en ander klein diertjies.

Massa	1 kg
Lengte (met stert)	62 cm
Moontlike lewensduur	15 jaar
Draagtyd	36 dae

ALLE NASIONALE PARKE

STRIPED POLECAT *Ictonyx striatus*

The polecat is mainly nocturnal in habit. Usually 2 to 3
young are born per litter. Well-known for the evil-smelling
liquid squirted from anal glands when attacked by an
enemy. It feeds on insects, rodents and other small
animals.

Mass	1 kg
Length (with tail)	62 cm
Potential longevity	15 years
Gestation period	36 days

ALL NATIONAL PARKS

LE PUTOIS RAYÉ *Ictonyx striatus*

Ce putois est essentiellement nocturne. Il est bien connu
pour le liquide malodorant (sécrété dans des glandes
anales) qu'il projette à distance sur ses adversaires. Il se
nourrit d'insectes, de rongeurs et d'autres petits animaux.
Il y a généralement 2 ou 3 petits par portée.

Poids	1 kg
Longueur (avec la queue)	62 cm
Longévité	15 ans
Durée de la gestation	36 jours

TOUS LES PARCS NATIONAUX

GESTREIFTER ILTIS *Ictonyx striatus*

Der Iltis ist hauptsächlich ein Nachttier. Er ist durch die über-
riechende Flüssigkeit bekannt, die er aus den Analdrüsen
spritzt, wenn er von einem Feind angegriffen wird. Er nährt
sich von Insekten, Nagetieren und anderem Getier.
Meistens werden 2 bis 3 Junge pro Wurf geboren.

Gewicht	1 kg
Länge (mit Schwanz)	62 cm
MöglicheLebensdauer	15 Jahre
Trächtigkeitszeit	36 Tage

IN ALLEN NATIONALPARKS

RATEL   *Mellivora capensis*

Die ratel is hoofsaaklik naglewend, maar kan wel in die vroeë oggend of laatmiddag opgemerk word. Dit is 'n vreeslose en taai mediumgroot karnivoor wat reptiele, voëls, klein soogdiere, aas, vrugte en veral heuning en byelarwes vreet. Van 1 tot 4 kleintjies per werpsel.

Massa	12 kg
Skouerhoogte	26 cm
Lengte (met stert)	95 cm
Moontlike lewensduur	24 jaar
Draagtyd	6 maande

**KRUGER/
TSITSIKAMMA/
KAROO/
KALAHARI-GEMSBOK**

HONEY-BADGER   *Mellivora capensis*

The honey-badger is mainly nocturnal in habit but may be seen in early morning or late afternoon. It is a fearless and tough medium-sized carnivore which will take reptiles, birds, small mammals, carrion, fruit and especially honey and bee larvae. Litters of 1 to 4.

Mass	12 kg
Shoulder height	26 cm
Length (with tail)	95 cm
Potential longevity	24 years
Gestation period	6 months

**KRUGER/
TSITSIKAMMA/
KAROO/
KALAHARI GEMSBOK**

LE RATEL   *Mellivora capensis*

Le ratel a une activité essentiellement nocturne mais on le rencontre parfois tôt le matin ou en fin d'après-midi. C'est un carnivore intrépide, de taille moyenne, qui se nourrit de reptiles, d'oiseaux, de petits mammifères, de charognes, de fruits et surtout de miel et de larves d'abeilles. La femelle met bas de 1 à 4 petits.

Poids	12 kg
Hauteur au garrot	26 cm
Longueur (avec la queue)	95 cm
Longévité	24 ans
Durée de la gestation	6 mois

**KRUGER/
TSITSIKAMMA/
KAROO/
KALAHARI GEMSBOK**

HONIGDACHS   *Mellivora capensis*

Der Honigdachs ist ein Nachttier, das aber auch frühmorgens oder am späten Nachmittag zu sehen ist. Er ist ein furchtloser und kräftiger Fleischfresser mittlerer Größe, der sich von Reptilien, kleinen Tieren, Aas, Früchten und vor allem Honig und Bienenlarven nährt. Würfe bestehen aus 1 bis 4 Jungen.

Gewicht	12 kg
Schulterhöhe	26 cm
Länge (mit Schwanz)	95 cm
Mögliche Lebensdauer	24 Jahre
Trächtigkeitszeit	6 Monate

**KRUGER/
TSITSIKAMMA/
KAROO/
KALAHARI GEMSBOK**

GROOTOTTER *Aonyx capensis*

Word in die standhoudende strome en kuile van die
Nasionale Krugerwildtuin aangetref, maar ook in die
tussengety-water van die Tsitsikammaseekus Nasionale
Park. Dit lewe hoofsaaklik van krappe, vis, paddas, voëls
en voëleiers. Van 2 tot 5 kleintjies word gebore.

Massa . . . . .12 kg
Lengte (met stert) . . . . . . 135 cm
Moontlike lewensduur . . . . . 16 jaar
Draagtyd . . . . 9 weke

KRUGER/
GOLDEN GATE/
TSITSIKAMMA/
BONTEBOK/
KAROO

CLAWLESS OTTER *Aonyx capensis*

Present in the perennial streams and pools of the Kruger
National Park but also in the intertidal waters of the
Tsitsikamma Coastal National Park. Feeds mainly on crabs,
fish, frogs, birds and birds' eggs. Two to 5 young are born
per litter.

Mass . . . . 12 kg
Length (with tail) . . . . 135 cm
Potential longevity . . . . . . 16 years
Gestation period . . . . . . 9 weeks

KRUGER/
GOLDEN GATE/
TSITSIKAMMA/
BONTEBOK/
KAROO

LA LOUTRE A JOUES BLANCHES *Aonyx capensis*

On rencontre cette loutre dans les rivières et bassins du
Parc National Kruger qui ne s'assèchent pas, et également
dans la zone de balancement des marées du Parc National
de la Côte de Tsitsikamma. Elle se nourrit essentiellement
de crabes, de poissons, de grenouilles, d'oiseaux et d'oeufs.
La femelle met bas de 2 à 5 petits.

Poids . . . . .12 kg
Longueur (avec la queue) . . .135 cm
Longévité . . . . 16 ans
Durée de la gestation . . . . 63 jours

KRUGER/
GOLDEN GATE/
TSITSIKAMMA/
BONTEBOK/
KAROO

KAPOTTER *Aonyx capensis*

Das Tier wird in perennierenden Wasserläufen und Tümpeln
im Kruger Nationalpark angetroffen, aber auch in dem
Gebiet zwischen Hoch- und Niedrigwasser im Tsitsikamma
Coastal Nationalpark. Es ernährt sich hauptsächlich von
Krabben, Fischen, Fröschen, Vögeln und Vogeleiern. Pro
Wurf werden 2 bis 5 Junge geboren.

Gewicht . . . . .12 kg
Länge (mit Schwanz) . . . . .135 cm
Mögliche Lebensdauer . . 16 Jahre
Trächtigkeitszeit . . . . . . 9 Wochen

KRUGER/
GOLDEN GATE/
TSITSIKAMMA/
BONTEBOK/
KAROO

SIWET *Civettictis civetta*

'n Nagdier wat in die Nasionale Krugerwildtuin voorkom.
Die kop is klein met klein oortjies. Die kleur is geelgrys met
swart kolle; die bene is swart en daar is 'n swart riffel langs
die lengte van die rug af. Die stert is swart met kringe. Dit
vang insekte, reptiele en klein soogdiertjies, maar vreet ook
graag aas en wilde vrugte. Van 2 tot 4 kleintjies word per
werpsel gebore.

Massa	10 kg
Hoogte by rugkurwe	38 cm
Lengte (met stert)	130 cm
Draagtyd	9 weke

KRUGER

CIVET *Civettictis civetta*

A nocturnal animal found in the Kruger National Park.
The head is small with short ears. The basic colour is
yellowish-grey with black spots; the legs are black and there
is a ridge of black hair along the length of the spine. The tail
is black with white rings. Feeds on insects, reptiles and
small mammals but also partial to carrion and wild fruit.
From 2 to 4 young are born per litter.

Mass	10 kg
Height (at arch of back)	38 cm
Length (with tail)	130 cm
Gestation period	9 weeks

KRUGER

LA CIVETTE *Civettictis civetta*

Un animal nocturne que l'on trouve dans le Parc National
Kruger. La tête est petite avec des oreilles courtes. Le
pelage est gris-jaune avec des taches noires; les pattes
sont noires et il y a une raie de poils noirs le long de la
colonne vertébrale. La queue est noire avec des anneaux
blancs. Cet animal se nourrit d'insectes, de reptiles et de
petits mammifères. Il aime aussi les charognes et les fruits
sauvages. La mère met bas de 2 à 4 petits.

Poids	10 kg
Hauteur (à la bosse dorsale)	38 cm
Longueur (avec la queue)	130 cm
Durée de la gestation	62 jours

KRUGER

ZIBETKATZE *Civettictis civetta*

Ein Nachttier, das im Kruger Nationalpark vorkommt. Der
Kopf ist klein, die Ohren sind kurz. Die Grundfarbe ist
gelblich-grau mit schwarzen Flecken. Die Beine sind
schwarz und über den Kamm führt ein schwarzes Band.
Der Schwanz ist schwarz mit weißen Ringen. Es nährt sich
von Insekten, Reptilien und kleinen Säugetieren. Die
Lieblingsgerichte sind Aas und wilde Früchte. Pro Wurf
werden 2 bis 4 Junge geboren.

Gewicht	10 kg
Höhe (in der Rückenwölbung)	38 cm
Länge (mit Schwanz)	130 cm
Trächtigkeitszeit	9 Wochen

KRUGER

KLEINKOLMUSKEJAATKAT *Genetta genetta*

Verskil van die grootkolmuskejaatkat vanweë die kolle wat gewoonlik kleiner is en die stert wat 'n wit punt het (nie swart nie). Dit vang klein soogdiertjies en voëls en is veral lief om kuikens uit neste te verwyder. Gewoonlik word 3 kleintjies per werpsel gebore.

Massa . . . . 2 kg
Lengte (met stert) . . . . 95 cm
Moontlike lewensduur . . . . . 13 jaar
Draagtyd . . . . .70 dae

KRUGER/BERGKWAGGA/ ADDO/TSITSIKAMMA/ BONTEBOK/KAROO/ KALAHARI-GEMSBOK/ LANGEBAAN

SMALL-SPOTTED GENET *Genetta genetta*

Differs from the large-spotted genet in that the spots are usually smaller, and in having a white-tipped (not black-tipped) tail. Preys on small mammals and birds, and is particularly fond of nestlings. Generally 3 young are born per litter.

Mass . . . . 2 kg
Length (with tail) . . . . 95 cm
Potential longevity . . . . . . 13 years
Gestation period . . . . 70 days

KRUGER/MOUNTAIN ZEBRA/ ADDO/TSITSIKAMMA/ BONTEBOK/KAROO/ KALAHARI GEMSBOK/ LANGEBAAN

LA GENETTE COMMUNE *Genetta genetta*

Elle se distingue de la genette à grandes taches par des taches plus petites et le bout de la queue blanc (et non pas noir). Sa nourriture se compose de petits mammifères, d'oiseaux et elle apprécie tout particulièrement les oiseaux nouveau-nés. La femelle donne généralement le jour à 3 jeunes.

Poids . . . . 2 kg
Longueur (avec la queue) . . . 95 cm
Longévité . . . . 13 ans
Gestation . . . . 70 jours

KRUGER/ ZÈBRE DE MONTAGNE/ ADDO/TSITSIKAMMA/ BONTEBOK/KAROO/ KALAHARI GEMSBOK/ LANGEBAAN

KLEINGEFLECKTE GINSTERKATZE *Genetta genetta*

Das Tier unterscheidet sich von der großen braun gefleckten Ginsterkatze dadurch, daß die Flecken meistens kleiner sind und der Schwanz eine weiße Spitze hat - und keine schwarze. Es nährt sich von kleinen Säugetieren und Vögeln, am liebsten von Nestlingen. Gewöhnlich werden 3 Junge geboren.

Gewicht . . . . 2 kg
Länge (mit Schwanz) . . . . . . 95 cm
Mögliche Lebensdauer . . . 13 Jahre
Trächtigkeitszeit . . . . .70 Tage

KRUGER/MOUNTAIN ZEBRA/ ADDO/TSITSIKAMMA/ BONTEBOK/KAROO/ KALAHARI GEMSBOK/ LANGEBAAN

KOMMETJIEGATMUISHOND *Atilax paludinosus*

Leef tussen die riete en plante langs riviere en damme.
Gewoonlik donkerbruin van kleur. Vlug die water in as dit
agtervolg word. Dit vang vis, paddas, krappe, insekte,
slange, voëls en vreet graag eiers. Twee kleintjies word per
werpsel gebore.

Massa	3,5 kg
Lengte (met stert)	90 cm

KRUGER/
GOLDEN GATE/
BERGKWAGGA/
ADDO/TSITSIKAMMA/
BONTEBOK/
LANGEBAAN

WATER MONGOOSE *Atilax paludinosus*

Frequents reeds and other vegetation margining rivers and
dams. Usually dark brown in colour. Takes readily to water
when pursued. Feeds on fish, frogs, crabs, insects, snakes
and birds, and is partial to birds' eggs. Two young are
usually born per litter.

Mass	3,5 kg
Length (with tail)	90 cm

KRUGER/
GOLDEN GATE/
MOUNTAIN ZEBRA/
ADDO/TSITSIKAMMA/
BONTEBOK/
LANGEBAAN

LA MANGOUSTE AQUATIQUE *Atilax paludinosus*

Elle vit dans les roseaux et autres herbes le long des
rivières et des barrages. Généralement de couleur brun
foncé. Elle saute rapidement à l'eau quand elle est
poursuivie. Elle se nourrit de grenouilles, de crabes,
d'insectes, de serpents et d'oiseaux, et elle est friande
d'oeufs d'oiseaux. La femelle met généralement bas 2
petits par portée.

Poids	3,5 kg
Longueur (avec la queue) . . .	90 cm

KRUGER/
GOLDEN GATE/
ZÈBRE DE MONTAGNE/
ADDO/TSITSIKAMMA/
BONTEBOK/
LANGEBAAN

WASSERMUNGO *Atilax paludinosus*

Hält sich im Schilf und zwischen anderen Pflanzen, die an
den Ufern von Flüssen und Teichen wachsen, auf. Die
Farbe des Tieres ist gewöhnlich dunkelbraun. Es taucht ins
Wasser, wenn es verfolgt wird. Es lebt von Fischen,
Fröschen, Krabben, Insekten, Schlangen und Vögeln. Die
Lieblingsnahrung sind Vogeleier. Meistens werden 2 Junge
pro Wurf geboren.

Gewicht	3,5 kg
Länge (mit Schwanz)	90 cm

KRUGER/
GOLDEN GATE/
MOUNTAIN ZEBRA/
ADDO/TSITSIKAMMA/
BONTEBOK/
LANGEBAAN

DWERGMUISHOND *Helogale parvula*

'n Klein donkerkleurige kuddediertjie wat bedags aktief is en snags in tonnels en gate in termietneste of boomstompe woon. Dit vreet insekte, reptiele en klein soogdiertjies. Word gewoonlik in groepe van 20 of meer aangetref.

```
Massa . . . . . . . . . . . . . .300 g
Lengte (met stert) . . . . . . . 40 cm
Draagtyd  . . . . . . . . . . . 52 dae
```

KRUGER

DWARF MONGOOSE *Helogale parvula*

A small dark-coloured gregarious animal which is active by day and shelters by night in old tunnels and holes in termite-mounds and tree-trunks. Feeds on insects, reptiles and small mammals. Generally found in groups of 20 or more.

```
Mass  . . . . . . . . . . . . . . 300 g
Length (with tail) . . . . . . . . 40 cm
Gestation period  . . . . . . . 52 days
```

KRUGER

LA MANGOUSTE NAINE *Helogale parvula*

C'est un petit animal grégaire, à la robe sombre et qui passe la nuit dans de vieux tunnels et trous dans des termitières ou dans des troncs d'arbres. Elle se nourrit d'insectes, de reptiles et de petits mammifères. On les rencontre généralement en groupes de vingt ou plus.

```
Poids . . . . . . . . . . . . . .300 g
Longueur (avec la queue)  . . . 40 cm
Durée de la gestation  . . . . 52 jours
```

KRUGER

ZWERGMUNGO *Helogale parvula*

Ein kleines dunkel gefärbtes Herdentier, das tagsüber aktiv ist und nachts in Tunneln und Löchern in Termitenbauen und Baumstämmen unterschlüpft. Es lebt von Insekten, Reptilien und kleinen Säugetieren. Es kommt gewöhnlich in Gruppen von mehr als 20 vor.

```
Gewicht . . . . . . . . . . . . . 300 g
Länge (mit Schwanz) . . . . . . 40 cm
Trächtigkeitszeit  . . . . . . . 52 Tage
```

KRUGER

GEBANDE MUISHOND *Mungos mungo*

Dit vreet insekte, akkedisse, voëls en klein soogdiertjies. Kenmerkend is die reeks van 12 tot 15 swart dwarsstrepe oor die rug. Jag dikwels saam met bobbejane op soek na insekte. Hierdie kuddedier word in groot troppe van 5 tot 60 diere aangetref, veral in klipperige omgewings.

Massa	1,5 kg
Lengte (met stert)	60 cm
Moontlike lewensduur	13 jaar
Draagtyd	60 dae

KRUGER

BANDED MONGOOSE *Mungos mungo*

Preys on insects, lizards, birds and small mammals. Characterized by series of 12 to 15 transverse black bands across its back. Often found hunting for insects in the company of baboons. It is gregarious and moves about in large packs of 5 to 60 animals, generally in stony areas.

Mass	1,5 kg
Length (with tail)	60 cm
Potential longevity	13 years
Gestation period	60 days

KRUGER

LA MANGOUSTE ZÈBRÉE *Mungos mungo*

Elle se nourrit d'insectes, de lézards, d'oiseaux et de petits mammifères. On la reconnait aux 12 à 15 rayures noires transversales sur son dos. Elle chasse souvent les insectes en compagnie de babouins. Ces mangoustes sont grégaires et se déplacent en groupes de 5 à 60 individus, fréquemment dans des zones rocheuses.

Poids	1,5 kg
Longueur (avec la queue)	60 cm
Longévité	13 ans
Durée de la gestation	60 jours

KRUGER

ZEBRAMANGUSTE *Mungos mungo*

Das Tier lebt von Insekten, Eidechsen, Vögeln und kleinen Säugetieren. Charakteristisch sind die 12 bis 15 schwarzen Streifen rund um den Rücken. Man trifft es oft in Gesellschaft von Pavianen bei der Insektenjagd an. Es ist ein Herdentier, das sich meistens in Gruppen von 5 bis 60 Tieren befindet und in steinigen Gegenden vorkommt.

Gewicht	1,5 kg
Länge	60 cm
Mögliche Lebensdauer	13 Jahre
Trächtigkeitszeit	60 Tage

KRUGER

ROOIMEERKAT *Cynictis penicillata*

Vang insekte, muise, voëls en vreet graag eiers. Gewoonlik word 2 (maar tot 5) kleintjies per werpsel gebore. Alhoewel hierdie meerkat gewoonlik alleen gesien word, woon dit in 'n trop van 5 tot 20 ander meerkatte. Bedags aktief.

Massa . . . . .600 g
Lengte (met stert) . . . . 50 cm
Moontlike lewensduur . . . . . 13 jaar

**GOLDEN GATE/
BERGKWAGGA/
ADDO/BONTEBOK/
KAROO/AUGRABIES/
KALAHARI-GEMSBOK/
LANGEBAAN**

YELLOW MONGOOSE *Cynictis penicillata*

Preys on insects, mice and birds and is fond of eggs. Generally 2 (but up to 5) young are born per litter. Although usually seen alone, this mongoose lives communally with 5 to 20 others. Active by day.

Mass . . . . 600 g
Length (with tail) . . . . 50 cm
Potential longevity . . . . . . 13 years

**GOLDEN GATE/
MOUNTAIN ZEBRA/
ADDO/BONTEBOK/
KAROO/AUGRABIES/
KALAHARI GEMSBOK/
LANGEBAAN**

LA MANGOUSTE JAUNE *Cynictis penicillata*

Elle se nourrit d'insectes, de souris et d'oiseaux et est très friande d'oeufs. La femelle met généralement bas 2 jeunes (mais parfois jusqu'à 5). Bien qu'on les voie souvent seules, ces mangoustes vivent en sociétés de 5 à 20 individus. Elles sont diurnes.

Poids . . . . .600 g
Longueur (avec la queue) . . . 50 cm
Longévité . . . . 13 ans

**GOLDEN GATE/
ZÈBRE DE MONTAGNE/
ADDO/BONTEBOK/
KAROO/AUGRABIES/
KALAHARI GEMSBOK/
LANGEBAAN**

FUCHSMANGUSTE *Cynictis penicillata*

Die Fuchsmanguste ernährt sich von Insekten, Mäusen und Vögeln. Sie frißt gerne Eier. Obwohl sie meistens allein gesehen wird, lebt diese Mangustenart in Gruppen von 5 bis 20. Sie ist am Tage aktiv. Gewöhnlich werden pro Wurf 2 (und höchstens 5) Junge geboren.

Gewicht . . . . .600 g
Länge (mit Schwanz) . . . . . . 50 cm
Mögliche Lebensdauer . . . . 13 Jahre

**GOLDEN GATE/
MOUNTAIN ZEBRA/
ADDO/BONTEBOK/
KAROO/AUGRABIES/
KALAHARI GEMSBOK/
LANGEBAAN**

STOKSTERTMEERKAT *Suricata suricatta*

Kom algemeen in die Kalahari-gemsbok- en Bergkwagga nasionale parke voor. Dit woon in gate en word gewoonlik in groepies van 6 tot so veel as 40 aangetref. Bedags aktief. Twee tot 3 kleintjies word gebore. Vreet hoofsaaklik insekte, maar ook reptiele en voëls.

Massa	.750 g
Lengte (met stert)	55 cm
Moontlike lewensduur	13 jaar
Draagtyd	10 weke

**BERGKWAGGA/
ADDO/KAROO/
KALAHARI-GEMSBOK**

SURICATE *Suricata suricatta*

Found commonly in the Kalahari Gemsbok and Mountain Zebra national parks. It inhabits burrows and is usually found in groups of 6 or more - sometimes up to 40. Active by day. Two to 3 young are born at a time. Feeds mainly on insects, but also on reptiles and birds.

Mass	750 g
Length (with tail)	55 cm
Potential longevity	13 years
Gestation period	10 weeks

**MOUNTAIN ZEBRA/
ADDO/KAROO/
KALAHARI GEMSBOK**

LE SURICATE *Suricata suricatta*

Il est très répandu dans le Parc National Kalahari Gemsbok et dans le Parc National du Zèbre de Montagne. Il vit dans des terriers et généralement en groupes de 6 ou plus (parfois jusqu'à 40). C'est un animal diurne qui se nourrit surtout d'insectes mais également de reptiles et d'oiseaux. La femelle met bas 2 ou 3 petits.

Poids	.750 g
Longueur (avec la queue)	55 cm
Longévité	13 ans
Durée de la gestation	70 jours

**ZÈBRE DE MONTAGNE/
ADDO/KAROO/
KALAHARI GEMSBOK**

ERDMÄNNCHEN *Suricata suricatta*

Das Erdmännchen ist häufig im Kalahari Gemsbok- und im Mountain Zebra Nationalpark anzutreffen. Es lebt in Bauen, gewöhnlich in Gruppen von 6 oder mehr - manchmal bis zu 40. Es ist tagsüber aktiv. Zwei bis 3 Junge werden geboren. Es nährt sich meist von Insekten, aber auch von Reptilien und Vögeln.

Gewicht	750 g
Länge	55 cm
Mögliche Lebensdauer	13 Jahre
Trächtigkeitszeit	.10 Wochen

**MOUNTAIN ZEBRA/
ADDO/KAROO/
KALAHARI GEMSBOK**

ERDVARK *Orycteropus afer*

'n Nagdier wat van rysmiere lewe en bekend is vir gate grawe. Dit word in die meeste van ons parke aangetref. 'n Enkele kleintjie word gebore.

Massa	.55 kg
Lengte (met stert)	170 cm
Moontlike lewensduur	10 jaar
Draagtyd	7 maande

**KRUGER/
BERGKWAGGA/
ADDO/KAROO/
AUGRABIES/
KALAHARI-GEMSBOK/
LANGEBAAN**

AARDVARK *Orycteropus afer*

A nocturnal animal which feeds on termites. It is noted for its burrowing powers, and is found in most of our parks. A single young is born at a time.

Mass	55 kg
Length (with tail)	170 cm
Potential longevity	10 years
Gestation period	7 months

**KRUGER/
MOUNTAIN ZEBRA/
ADDO/KAROO/
AUGRABIES/
KALAHARI GEMSBOK/
LANGEBAAN**

L'ORYCTÉROPE *Orycteropus afer*

Cet animal nocturne se nourrit de termites. Il est connu pour son habileté à creuser. On le trouve dans la plupart de nos parcs. La femelle ne met bas qu'un petit à la fois.

Poids	.55 kg
Longueur (avec la queue)	.170 cm
Longévité	10 ans
Durée de la gestation	7 mois

**KRUGER/
ZÈBRE DE MONTAGNE/
ADDO/ KAROO/
AUGRABIES/
KALAHARI GEMSBOK/
LANGEBAAN**

ERDFERKEL *Orycteropus afer*

Ein Nachttier, das sich von Termiten ernährt. Es ist bekannt für seine Fähigkeit, Baue zu graben, und kommt in den meisten unserer Parks vor. Ein einziges Junges wird geboren.

Gewicht	.55 kg
Länge (mit Schwanz)	.170 cm
Mögliche Lebensdauer	10 Jahre
Trächtigkeitszeit	7 Monate

**KRUGER/
MOUNTAIN ZEBRA/
ADDO/ KAROO/
AUGRABIES/
KALAHARI GEMSBOK/
LANGEBAAN**

OLIFANT *Loxodonta africana*

Hulle kom veral in die noordelike deel van die Nasionale Krugerwildtuin voor. In die Addo-olifant Nasionale Park is daar nou 135 olifante, nadat dit in die twintigerjare slegs 11 gehad het. Die olifante is ietwat kleiner, het swak ontwikkelde of geen tande nie, hulle ore vertoon meer ovaal as die van ander, en hulle vreet hoofsaaklik spekboom. Wanneer die kalfie aan sy moeder drink, gebruik hy sy bek, maar water word met die slurp opgesuig en in die bek gespuit. Twee spene is tussen die voorbene geleë. Puberteit begin gewoonlik op die elfde jaar.

Massa (bul)	5 500 kg
Skouerhoogte (bul)	4,0 m
Moontlike lewensduur	60 jaar
Draagtyd	.22 maande
Loopsnelheid	10 km/h
Stormsnelheid	40 km/h

KRUGER/ADDO

AFRICAN ELEPHANT *Loxodonta africana*

Particularly abundant in the northern section of the Kruger National Park. In the Addo Elephant National Park there are now 135 elephants - up from a low point of 11 in the 1920s. The Addo elephant is slightly smaller, its tusks are absent or poorly developed, its ears appear to be more oval, and it feeds mainly on spekboom. When it suckles the calf uses its mouth, but water is sucked up in the trunk and squirted into the mouth. Two mammae are situated between the mother's forelegs. Puberty is reached at approximately 11 years of age.

Mass (male)	5 500 kg
Shoulder height (male)	.4,0 m
Potential longevity	60 years
Gestation period	22 months
Walking speed	10 km/h
Charging speed	40 km/h

KRUGER/ADDO

L'ÉLÉPHANT AFRICAIN *Loxodonta africana*

Il est particulièrement répandu dans le nord du Parc National Kruger. Il y a 135 éléphants dans le Parc National Addo des Éléphants (il n'y en avait plus que 11 dans les années vingt). L'éléphant d'Addo est plus petit; ses défenses sont peu développées ou inexistantes; ses oreilles semblent plus ovales et il se nourrit surtout de 'spekboom'. Pendant l'allaitement le jeune utilise sa gueule, mais l'eau est aspirée par la trompe et aspergée dans la gueule. Les femelles ont 2 mamelles entre les pattes de devant. L'éléphant atteint la puberté à environ 11 ans.

Poids du mâle	5 500 kg
Hauteur au garrot (mâle)	.4,0 m
Longévité	60 ans
Durée de la gestation	22 mois
Vitesse de marche	10 km/h
Vitesse de charge	40 km/h

KRUGER/ADDO

AFRIKANISCHER ELEFANT *Loxodonta africana*

Im nördlichen Teil des Kruger Nationalparks gibt es viele Elefanten. Im Addo Elephant Nationalpark leben jetzt 135 Elefanten, während es dort in den zwanziger Jahren nur 11 gab. Die Addo-Elefanten sind etwas kleiner als ihre Vettern im Norden. Sie beshabeitzen keine Stoßzähne, oder diese sind nur kümmerlich entwickelt. Wenn das Kalb an seiner Mutter trinkt, tut es dies mit dem Mund. Aber Wasser wird in den Rüssel gesaugt und dann in den Mund gespritzt. Das Euter liegt zwischen den Vorderbeinen der Mutter. Die Pubertät beginnt mit 11 Jahren.

Gewicht (Männchen)	5 500 kg
Schulterhöhe (Männchen)	.4,0 m
Lebensdauer	60 Jahre
Trächtigkeitszeit	22 Monate
Schrittschnelligkeit	10 km/h
Angriffsschnelligkeit	40 km/h

KRUGER/ADDO

KLIPDASSIE *Procavia capensis*

Die klipdassie verkies om in klipskeure en rotse skuiling te vind en is plantvretend. Bedags aktief. Twee tot 3 kleintjies word per werpsel gebore.

Massa	3-4 kg
Lengte	50 cm
Moontlike lewensduur	7 jaar
Draagtyd	7,5 maande

**KRUGER/GOLDEN GATE/
BERGKWAGGA/ ADDO/
TSITSIKAMMA/BONTEBOK/
KAROO/AUGRABIES/
LANGEBAAN**

ROCK DASSIE *Procavia capensis*

The rock dassie prefers to live in rock fissures and among boulders. It is herbivorous. It is active by day. Two to 3 young are born per litter.

Mass	3-4 kg
Length	50 cm
Potential longevity	7 years
Gestation period	7,5 months

**KRUGER/GOLDEN GATE/
MOUNTAIN ZEBRA/ADDO/
TSITSIKAMMA/BONTEBOK/
KAROO/AUGRABIES/
LANGEBAAN**

LE DAMAN DES ROCHERS *Procavia capensis*

Le daman préfère vivre dans les anfractuosités des rochers et entre les gros rochers. C'est un animal herbivore et diurne. La femelle met bas 2 ou 3 jeunes par portée.

Poids	3-4 kg
Longueur	50 cm
Longévité	7 ans
Durée de la gestation	7,5 mois

**KRUGER/GOLDEN GATE/
ZÈBRE DE MONTAGNE/
ADDO/TSITSIKAMMA/
BONTEBOK/KAROO/
AUGRABIES/LANGEBAAN**

KAPKLIPSCHLIEFER *Procavia capensis*

Der Klipschliefer lebt in Felsspalten oder zwischen Felsblöcken. Er frißt Pflanzen. Er ist am Tage aktiv. Pro Wurf werden 2 bis 3 Junge geboren.

Gewicht	3-4 kg
Länge	50 cm
Mögliche Lebensdauer	7 Jahre
Trächtigkeitszeit	7,5 Monate

**KRUGER/GOLDEN GATE/
MOUNTAIN ZEBRA/
ADDO/TSITSIKAMMA/
BONTEBOK/KAROO/
AUGRABIES/ LANGEBAAN**

SWARTRENOSTER *Diceros bicornis*

Die swartrenoster het 'n verlengde, effens gepunte bolip wat oor die onderlip strek. Dit is donkergrys van kleur. Dit het uit die Nasionale Krugerwildtuin verdwyn en in die Addo-gebied uitgesterf, maar is weer in beide ingevoer, asook in die Vaalbos en Augrabieswaterval nasionale parke. Die Addo-renoster, waarvan daar nou 18 is, kom van die subspesie uit Kenia. 'n Enkele kalfie word gebore.

Massa	1 000 kg
Skouerhoogte	160 cm
Snelheid	45 km/h
Voorste horinglengterekord	. 120 cm
Tweede horinglengterekord	. 44,5 cm
Moontlike lewensduur	. . . . 45 jaar
Draagtyd	15 maande

KRUGER/ADDO/AUGRABIES

BLACK RHINOCEROS *Diceros bicornis*

The black rhinoceros is characterized by an elongated slightly pointed upper lip overlapping the lower. It is dark grey in colour. Extinct in Kruger and Addo Elephant national parks, but has been reintroduced into both, as well as to Vaalbos and Augrabies Falls national parks. The Addo rhinoceroses are of the Kenyan subspecies and now number 18. A single calf is the rule.

Mass	1 000 kg
Shoulder height	. 160 cm
Running speed	45 km/h
Record front horn length	120 cm
Record rear horn length	44,5 cm
Potential longevity	. . . 45 years
Gestation period	. . . . 15 months

KRUGER/ADDO/AUGRABIES

LE RHINOCÉROS NOIR *Diceros bicornis*

On reconnait le rhinocéros noir à sa lèvre supérieure allongée et un peu pointue, qui chevauche la lèvre inférieure. Il est de couleur gris foncé. Il avait disparu dans les parcs nationaux Kruger et Addo des Éléphants, mais y a été réintroduit, ainsi que dans les parcs de Vaalbos et d'Augrabies. Les rhinocéros de l'Addo appartiennent à la sous-espèce kenyenne et sont maintenant au nombre de 18. La femelle ne donne généralement naissance qu'à un petit.

Poids	1 000 kg
Hauteur au garrot	160 cm
Vitesse de course	45 km/h
Longueur record de la corne avant	120 cm
Longueur record de la corne arrière	44,5 cm
Longévité	. . . . 45 ans
Durée de la gestation	. . . 15 mois

KRUGER/ADDO/AUGRABIES

SPITZNASHORN *Diceros bicornis*

Das Spitznashorn ist durch eine verlängerte leicht zugespitzte Oberlippe charakterisiert, die über die Unterlippe herüberhängt. Es ist dunkelgrau gefärbt. Dieses Tier war im Kruger- und auch im Addo Elephant Nationalpark ausgestorben, wurde aber in beiden Wildreservaten als auch im Vaalbos- und Augrabies Falls Nationalpark wieder heimisch gemacht. Die Addo-Nashörner, von denen es heute 18 gibt, kommen aus Kenia. Ein einziges Kalb wird normalerweise geboren.

Gewicht	1 000 kg
Schulterhöhe	160 cm
Laufschnelligkeit	45 km/h
Rekordlänge des vorderen Horns	120 cm
Rekordlänge des hinteren Horns	44,5 cm
Mögliche Lebensdauer	. . 45 Jahre
Trächtigkeitszeit	. . . . . 15 Monate

KRUGER/ADDO/AUGRABIES

WITRENOSTER *Ceratotherium simum*

Die witrenoster word gekenmerk deur sy plat, breë bolip en nie sodanig deur sy ligte kleur nie, alhoewel dit gewoonlik ligter as die swartrenoster is. Dit het uit die Nasionale Krugerwildtuin verdwyn, maar is weer ingevoer in 1961. 'n Enkele kalfie word gebore.

Massa (bul)	2 150 kg
Skouerhoogte (bul)	180 cm
Snelheid	40 km/h
Voorste horinglengterekord	158 cm
Tweede horinglengterekord	56,6 cm
Moontlike lewensduur	45 jaar
Draagtyd	16 maande

KRUGER

WHITE RHINOCEROS *Ceratotherium simum*

The white rhinoceros is characterized chiefly by its broad, square upper lip, and not essentially by its lighter colour although it is usually more grey than the black rhinoceros. Disappeared from the Kruger National Park, but was reintroduced in 1961. A single calf is the rule.

Mass (male)	2 150 kg
Shoulder height	180 cm
Running speed	40 km/h
Record front horn length	158 cm
Record rear horn length	56,6 cm
Potential longevity	45 years
Gestation period	16 months

KRUGER

LE RHINOCÉROS BLANC *Ceratotherium simum*

On reconnait le rhinocéros blanc surtout à sa lèvre supérieure large et carrée et non pas essentiellement à sa couleur plus pâle (bien qu'il soit d'habitude d'un gris moins sombre que le rhinocéros noir). Il a disparu du Parc National Kruger, mais y a été reintroduit en 1961. La femelle ne donne généralement naissance qu'à un petit.

Poids du mâle	2 150 kg
Hauteur au garrot	180 cm
Vitesse	40 km/h
Longueur record de la corne avant	158 cm
Longueur record de la corne arrière	56,6 cm
Longévité	45 ans
Durée de la gestation	16 mois

KRUGER

BREITMAULNASHORN *Ceratotherium simum*

Das Breitmaulnashorn ist hauptsächlich durch seine breite, viereckige Oberlippe und nicht notwendigerweise durch seine lichtere Färbung charakterisiert, obwohl es meistens grauer ist als das Spitznashorn. Es war im Kruger Nationalpark ausgestorben, wurde dort aber 1961 wieder eingeführt. In der Regel wird ein einziges Kalb geboren.

Gewicht (Männchen)	2 150 kg
Schulterhöhe	180 cm
Schnelligkeit	40 km/h
Rekordlänge des vorderen Horns	158 cm
Rekordlänge des hinteren Horns	56,6 cm
Mögliche Lebensdauer	45 Jahre
Trächtigkeitszeit	16 Monate

KRUGER

BERGKWAGGA *Equus zebra*

Die bergkwagga kom voor in die Bergkwagga Nasionale
Park en is onlangs in die Karoo Nasionale Park ingevoer.
Anders as by die bontkwagga is daar 'n duidelike keelvel
aanwesig en daar is 'n ruitpatroon bo-op die kruis bokant
die stert. Daar is ook geen skadustrepe nie en die strepe
reik nie om die pens nie. Die strepe op die bene is duidelik
sigbaar tot op die hoewe, en strek reg om die bene.
'n Enkele vulletjie word gebore.

Massa	250 kg
Skouerhoogte	130 cm
Snelheid	65 km/h
Moontlike lewensduur	35 jaar
Draagtyd	12 maande

BERGKWAGGA/KAROO

MOUNTAIN ZEBRA *Equus zebra*

Found in the Mountain Zebra National Park and recently
re-established in the Karoo National Park. Differs from
Burchell's zebra in that a definite dewlap is present and
there is a 'grid-iron' stripe pattern on the top of the rump
above the tail. There are also no 'shadow' stripes between
the black body stripes and the stripes do not meet on the
underside of the body. The stripes on the legs extend
clearly down to the hoofs and encircle the legs. A single foal
is born.

Mass	250 kg
Shoulder height	130 cm
Speed	65 km/h
Potential longevity	35 years
Gestation period	12 months

MOUNTAIN ZEBRA/KAROO

LE ZÈBRE DE MONTAGNE *Equus zebra*

On le trouve dans le Parc National du Zèbre de Montagne et
il a récemment été réintroduit dans le Parc National du
Karoo. Il se distingue du zèbre de Burchell par la présence
d'un net fanon et par le motif en 'grille' au sommet de la
croupe et sur le dessus de la queue. Il n'a pas non plus de
'bandes d'ombres' entre les bandes noires. En outre, les
bandes noires ne font pas le tour du corps. Les bandes des
pattes sont nettement marquées jusqu'aux sabots et font le
tour entier des pattes. La femelle met bas un seul jeune.

Poids	250 kg
Hauteur au garrot	130 cm
Vitesse	65 km/h
Longévité	35 ans
Durée de la gestation	12 mois

ZÈBRE DE MONTAGNE/KAROO

BERGZEBRA *Equus zebra*

Es kommt im Mountain Zebra Nationalpark vor und wurde
kürzlich in den Karoo Nationalpark eingeführt. Es unterscheidet sich vom Burchell-Zebra dadurch, daß es eine
deutliche Wamme hat. Oben auf dem Rumpf über dem
Schwanz ist ein Streifenmuster sichtbar. Weiterhin hat es
keine Schattenstreifen zwischen den schwarzen Streifen am
Körper. Die Streifen selbst gehen nicht um den ganzen
Körper. Die Streifen an den Beinen sind deutlich bis
hinunter zu den Hufen sichtbar und reichen um das ganze
Bein. Ein einziges Füllen wird geboren.

Gewicht	250 kg
Schulterhöhe	130 cm
Schnelligkeit	65 km/h
Mögliche Lebensdauer	35 Jahre
Trächtigkeitszeit	12 Monate

MOUNTAIN ZEBRA/KAROO

BONTKWAGGA *Equus burchellii*

Op die bontkwagga strek die strepe tot om die pens en daar is duidelike maar ligte skadustrepe tussenin. Anders as by die bergkwagga is die strepe op die bene slegs aan die buitekant sigbaar en van die knieë af ondertoe gewoonlik onduidelik. Daar is geen keelvel of ruitpatroon op die kruis nie. 'n Enkele vulletjie word gebore.

Massa	300 kg
Skouerhoogte	130 cm
Moontlike lewensduur	35 jaar
Draagtyd	12 maande

KRUGER/GOLDEN GATE

BURCHELL'S ZEBRA *Equus burchellii*

On this zebra the stripes reach right round the body and definite fainter 'shadow' stripes are present. Unlike the mountain zebra the stripes on the legs occur on the outside only and from the knees down they are usually indistinct. There is no dewlap and no 'grid-iron' pattern on the rump. A single foal is the rule.

Mass	300 kg
Shoulder height	130 cm
Potential longevity	35 years
Gestation period	12 months

KRUGER/GOLDEN GATE

LE ZÈBRE DE BURCHELL *Equus burchellii*

Sur ce zèbre les bandes font le tour du corps et on voit des 'bandes d'ombres' plus pâles, mais bien définies. Contrairement au zèbre de montagne, les bandes des pattes n'apparaissent qu'à l'extérieur et à partir du genou elles sont généralement peu nettes. Il y a ni fanon ni motif en 'grille' sur la croupe. La femelle n'a généralement qu'un petit.

Poids	300 kg
Hauteur au garrot	130 cm
Longévité	35 ans
Durée de la gestation	12 mois

KRUGER/GOLDEN GATE

BURCHELL-ZEBRA *Equus burchellii*

Bei diesem Zebra gehen die Streifen rund um den Körper und hellere Schattenstreifen sind deutlich sichtbar. Im Gegensatz zum Bergzebra kommen die Streifen an den Beinen nur an der Außenseite vor und vom Knie nach unten sind sie meistens undeutlich. Es gibt keine Wamme und kein Streifenmuster auf dem Rumpf. In der Regel wird ein einziges Füllen geboren.

Gewicht	300 kg
Schulterhöhe	130 cm
Mögliche Lebensdauer	35 Jahre
Trächtigkeitszeit	12 Monate

KRUGER/GOLDEN GATE

SEEKOEI *Hippopotamus amphibius*

Hierdie amfibiese soogdier hou in al die vernaamste riviere van die Nasionale Krugerwildtuin. 'n Enkele kleintjie word in 'n afgesonderde rietbedding naby water gebore. Gebiede word gemerk deur die seekoei se eienaardige gebruik om sy mis met vinnige bewegings van die stert oop te sprei.

Massa (bul)	1 500 kg
Skouerhoogte	150 cm
Lengte (kop en liggaam)	.3,7 m
Moontlike lewensduur	54 jaar
Draagtyd	8 maande

KRUGER

HIPPOPOTAMUS *Hippopotamus amphibius*

This amphibious mammal is found in all the large rivers of the Kruger National Park. A single young is born in a secluded reed-bed near water. Territories are marked by the hippo's peculiar habit of scattering its dung with rapid flicks of its tail.

Mass (male)	1 500 kg
Shoulder height	.150 cm
Length (head and body)	.3,7 m
Potential longevity	54 years
Gestation period	8 months

KRUGER

L'HIPPOPOTAME *Hippopotamus amphibius*

On rencontre ce mammifère amphibien dans les fleuves du Parc National Kruger. La femelle met bas un seul jeune dans un lit de roseaux retiré et à proximité de l'eau. L'hippopotame marque son territoire en étalant ses excréments à rapides coups de queue.

Poids du mâle	1 500 kg
Hauteur au garrot	150 cm
Longueur (tête et corps)	.3,7 m
Longévité	54 ans
Durée de la gestation	8 mois

KRUGER

FLUSSPFERD *Hippopotamus amphibius*

Dieses amphibische Säugetier wird in allen grossen Flüssen des Kruger Nationalparks angetroffen. Ein einziges Junges wird in einem versteckten Schilfbett in Wassernähe geboren. Das Flußpferd kennzeichnet sein Gebiet, indem es auf merkwürdige Art und Weise Mist mit dem Schwanz zerstreut.

Gewicht (Männchen)	.1 500 kg
Schulterhöhe	150 cm
Länge (Kopf und Rumpf)	.3,7 m
Mögliche Lebensdauer	54 Jahre
Trächtigkeitszeit	.8 Monate

KRUGER

VLAKVARK *Phacochoerus aethiopicus*

Rekordlengte van die boonste slagtande is 61 cm. Gewoonlik word 2-3 kleintjies per werpsel tussen September en Desember gebore. Kenmerkend is die 2 paar vratagtige uitgroeisels aan die kop van die beer (1 paar by die sog) en die penorente stert as hy hardloop. Bedags aktief.

Massa (beer)	.80 kg
Skouerhoogte	70 cm
Snelheid	30-50 km/h
Moontlike lewensduur	20 jaar
Draagtyd	170 dae

KRUGER/GOLDEN GATE

WARTHOG *Phacochoerus aethiopicus*

The record length of an upper tusk is 61 cm. A litter of usually 2 to 3 piglets is born between September and December. Characteristics are the 2 pairs of wartlike excrescences on the head of the male (1 pair in female) and the habit of holding its tail stiffly erect when running. Active by day.

Mass (male)	.80 kg
Shoulder height	70 cm
Speed	30-50 km/h
Potential longevity	20 years
Gestation period	170 days

KRUGER/GOLDEN GATE

LE PHACOCHÈRE *Phacochoerus aethiopicus*

La longueur record d'une défense supérieure est de 61 cm. Cet animal se distingue par 2 paires d'excroissances semblables à des verrues sur la tête du mâle (une paire chez la femelle) et par sa queue qui demeure à la verticale lorsqu'il court. Il est diurne. La femelle met généralement bas 2 ou 3 petits entre septembre et décembre.

Poids du mâle	80 kg
Hauteur au garrot	70 cm
Vitesse	30-50 km/h
Longévité	20 ans
Durée de la gestation	170 jours

KRUGER/GOLDEN GATE

WARZENSCHWEIN *Phacochoerus aethiopicus*

Die Rekordlänge des oberen Stoßzahnes ist 61 cm. Ein Wurf von meistens 2 bis 3 Jungen wird in den Monaten September bis Dezember geboren. Charakteristisch sind die zwei Paar warzenartigen Auswüchse am Kopf des Männchens (ein Paar beim Weibchen) sowie die Gewohnheit, den Schwanz beim Laufen steif in der Luft zu halten. Es ist tagsüber aktiv.

Gewicht	.80 kg
Schulterhöhe	70 cm
Schnelligkeit	30-50 km/h
Mögliche Lebensdauer	20 Jahre
Trächtigkeitszeit	.170 Tage

KRUGER/GOLDEN GATE

BOSVARK *Potamochoerus porcus*

Die onderste slagtande se rekordlengte is 18 cm.
Gewoonlik 2-4 kleintjies (maar soveel as 8) word per
werpsel gebore. 'n Nagdier met kenmerkende snoet.
Die bosvark is skaars en word selde in die Nasionale
Krugerwildtuin gesien, maar is meer algemeen in die
Addo-olifant en Tsitsikamma nasionale parke.

Massa . . . . .62 kg
Skouerhoogte . . . . 70 cm
Moontlike lewensduur . . . . . 20 jaar

**KRUGER/
BERGKWAGGA/
ADDO/
TSITSIKAMMA**

BUSHPIG *Potamochoerus porcus*

The record length of the lower tusk is 18 cm. Usually 2 to 4
young (but up to 8) are born per litter. A nocturnal animal
with characteristic snout. Rare, and seldom seen in the
Kruger National Park, but commoner in the Addo Elephant
and Tsitsikamma national parks.

Mass . . . . 62 kg
Shoulder height . . . . 70 cm
Potential longevity . . . . . . 20 years

**KRUGER/
MOUNTAIN ZEBRA/
ADDO/
TSITSIKAMMA**

LE POTAMOCHÈRE *Potamochoerus porcus*

La longueur record de la défense inférieure est de 18 cm.
C'est un animal nocturne avec un groin très caractéristique.
Il est peu répandu et rarement vu dans le Parc National
Kruger mais il est plus commun dans les parcs nationaux de
Tsitsikamma et dans le Parc National Addo. La femelle
donne généralement le jour à entre 2 et 4 petits (mais
parfois jusqu'à 8).

Poids . . . . .62 kg
Hauteur au garrot . . . . 70 cm
Longévité . . . . 20 ans

**KRUGER/
ZÈBRE DE MONTAGNE/
ADDO/
TSITSIKAMMA**

BUSCHSCHWEIN *Potamochoerus porcus*

Die Rekordlänge des unteren Stoßzahnes ist 18 cm.
Gewöhnlich werden 2 bis 4 (aber bis zu 6) Junge geboren.
Es ist ein Nachttier mit einer charakteristischen Schnauze.
Es ist selten und wird im Kruger Nationalpark wenig
gesehen. Im Addo Elephant- und Tsitsikamma Nationalpark
kommt es haüfiger vor.

Gewicht . . . . .62 kg
Schulterhöhe . . . . 70 cm
Mögliche Lebensdauer . . . 20 Jahre

**KRUGER/
MOUNTAIN ZEBRA/
ADDO/
TSITSIKAMMA**

KAMEELPERD *Giraffa camelopardalis*

Die kameelperd verkies taamlike oop bosveld en is besonder volop suid van die Olifantsrivier in die Nasionale Krugerwildtuin. 'n Enkele kalfie met 'n liggaamsmassa van ongeveer 100 kg en met 'n skouerhoogte van 150 cm word enige tyd van die jaar gebore.

Massa	1 200 kg
Hoogte (tot op kop)	3,9-5,2 m
Snelheid	50 km/h
Moontlike lewensduur	28 jaar
Draagtyd	15 maande

KRUGER

GIRAFFE *Giraffa camelopardalis*

A single calf with a body mass of about 100 kg and with a shoulder height of 150 cm is born at any time of the year. The species prefers fairly open bushveld, and is particularly abundant south of the Olifants River in the Kruger National Park.

Mass	1 200 kg
Height (top of head)	3,9-5,2 m
Speed	50 km/h
Potential longevity	28 years
Gestation period	15 months

KRUGER

LA GIRAFE *Giraffa camelopardalis*

Les girafes affectionnent les zones de brousse assez ouverte et sont particulièrement nombreuses au sud du fleuve Olifants dans le Parc National Kruger. La femelle donne naissance à un seul petit (qui pèse environ 100 kg et dont la hauteur au garrot est de 150 cm) à n'importe quelle époque de l'année.

Poids	1 200 kg
Hauteur totale	3,9-5,2 m
Vitesse	50 km/h
Longévité	28 ans
Durée de la gestation	15 mois

KRUGER

GIRAFFE *Giraffa camelopardalis*

Ein einziges Kalb von circa 100 kg und einer Schulterhöhe von 150 cm kann irgendwann im Laufe des Jahres geboren werden. Das Tier bevorzugt offenes Buschveld und kommt besonders häufig südlich vom Olifantsfluß im Kruger Nationalpark vor.

Gewicht	1 200 kg
Grösse (ohne Hörner)	3,9-5,2 m
Schnelligkeit	50 km/h
Mögliche Lebensdauer	28 Jahre
Trächtigkeitszeit	15 Monate

KRUGER

ROOIDUIKER *Cephalophus natalensis*

Die rooiduiker is rooibruin in kleur met ligter onderdele. In die Nasionale Krugerwildtuin word dit in bosryke streke naby water in die Nasionale Pretoriuskop-omgewing aangetref. Gewoonlik word 'n enkele lam gebore. Daar is geen vaste paartyd nie.

Massa	.14 kg
Skouerhoogte	43 cm
Rekordhoringlengte	10 cm
Moontlike lewensduur	.9 jaar

KRUGER

RED DUIKER *Cephalophus natalensis*

This species is reddish-brown in colour with lighter underparts. In the Kruger National Park it inhabits dense bush near water in the Pretoriuskop area. Usually a single lamb is born. There is no fixed breeding season.

Mass	14 kg
Shoulder height	43 cm
Record horn length	10 cm
Potential longevity	.9 years

KRUGER

LE CÉPHALOPHE ROUGE *Cephalophus natalensis*

Cette espèce est de couleur rouge tirant sur le brun, la partie inférieure du corps étant plus pâle. Dans le Parc National Kruger on le trouve dans la brousse dense, à proximité des points d'eau dans la région de Pretoriuskop. Il n'a pas de saison de reproduction fixe et la femelle ne met généralement bas qu'un seul petit.

Poids	.14 kg
Hauteur au garrot	43 cm
Longueur record des cornes	10 cm
Longévité	9 ans

KRUGER

ROTDUCKER *Cephalophus natalensis*

Das Tier ist rotbraun gefärbt. Der untere Teil des Körpers ist lichter. Im Kruger Nationalpark bewohnt es den dichten Busch in Wassernähe bei Pretoriuskop. Gewöhnlich wird ein einziges Kitz irgendwann im Jahr geboren.

Gewicht	.14 kg
Schulterhöhe	43 cm
Rekordlänge der Hörner	10 cm
Mögliche Lebensdauer	.9 Jahre

KRUGER

BLOUDUIKER *Philantomba monticola*

Die kleinste van ons antilope. Dit woon in die digte woude van die Suid- en Suidoos-Kaap, maar word ook in verskeie natuurreservate van Natal aangetref. Gewoonlik word 'n enkele lam in Oktober of November gebore.

Massa	4 kg
Skouerhoogte	30 cm
Rekordhoringlengte	5,7 cm
Moontlike lewensduur	9 jaar

TSITSIKAMMA

BLUE DUIKER *Philantomba monticola*

The smallest of our antelopes. It inhabits the forest regions of the south and south-eastern Cape but is also present in various nature reserves in Natal. Usually a single lamb is born in October or November.

Mass	4 kg
Shoulder height	30 cm
Record horn length	5,7 cm
Potential longevity	9 years

TSITSIKAMMA

LE CÉPHALOPHE BLEU *Philantomba monticola*

La plus petite de nos antilopes. Il peuple les régions forestières du sud et sud-est de la province du Cap, mais aussi diverses réserves de la province du Natal. La femelle met généralement bas un seul petit en octobre ou en novembre.

Poids	4 kg
Hauteur au garrot	30 cm
Longueur record des cornes	5,7 cm
Longévité	9 ans

TSITSIKAMMA

BLAUDUCKER *Philantomba monticola*

Die kleinste unserer Antilopen. Sie bewohnt die Waldgegenden des süd- und südöstlichen Kaplandes, aber sie kommt auch in verschiedenen Naturreservaten in Natal vor. Gewöhnlich wird ein einziges Kitz im Oktober oder November geboren.

Gewicht	4 kg
Schulterhöhe	30 cm
Rekordlänge der Hörner	5,7 cm
Mögliche Lebensdauer	9 Jahre

TSITSIKAMMA

GEWONE DUIKER *Sylvicapra grimmia*

Die gewone duiker is die mees algemene antiloop in Afrika.
Dit verkies oop bosveld waar dit skuiling kan vind in die
middel van die dag. 'n Enkele lam word gebore.

Massa	19 kg
Skouerhoogte	50 cm
Rekordhoringlengte	18 cm
Moontlike lewensduur	9 jaar
Draagtyd	3 maande

**KRUGER/BERGKWAGGA/
ADDO/BONTEBOK/
KAROO/AUGRABIES/
KALAHARI-GEMSBOK/
LANGEBAAN**

COMMON DUIKER *Sylvicapra grimmia*

The common duiker is the most widespread antelope in
Africa. It prefers open bush country where it can find cover
during the heat of the day. It produces one lamb at a birth.

Mass	19 kg
Shoulder height	50 cm
Record horn length	18 cm
Potential longevity	9 years
Gestation period	3 months

**KRUGER/MOUNTAIN ZEBRA/
ADDO/BONTEBOK/
KAROO/AUGRABIES/
KALAHARI GEMSBOK/
LANGEBAAN**

LE CÉPHALOPHE COMMUN *Sylvicapra grimmia*

Ce céphalophe (ou biche-cochon) est l'antilope la plus
commune d'Afrique. Elle habite les zones de la brousse où
elle peut s'abriter pendant les heures chaudes du jour. La
femelle met bas un petit.

Poids	19 kg
Hauteur au garrot	50 cm
Longueur record des cornes	18 cm
Longévité	9 ans
Durée de la gestation	3 mois

**KRUGER/
ZÈBRE DE MONTAGNE/
ADDO/BONTEBOK/KAROO/
AUGRABIES/KALAHARI
GEMSBOK/LANGEBAAN**

GEMEINER DUCKER *Sylvicapra grimmia*

Der Gemeine Ducker ist die am weitesten verbreitete
Antilope in Afrika. Er bevorzugt offenes Buschveld, wo er in
der Mittagshitze Unterschlupf findet. Es wird ein einziges
Kitz geboren.

Gewicht	19 kg
Schulterhöhe	50 cm
Rekordlänge der Hörner	18 cm
Mögliche Lebensdauer	9 Jahre
Trächtigkeitszeit	3 Monate

**KRUGER/MOUNTAIN ZEBRA/
ADDO/BONTEBOK/
KAROO/AUGRABIES/
KALAHARI GEMSBOK/
LANGEBAAN**

STEENBOK *Raphicerus campestris*

Kom in die meeste van ons nasionale parke voor, buiten die Addo- en Tsitsikammaparke. Slegs die mannetjie het horings. Hulle is aktief vroeg in die dag en weer laat in die middag. 'n Enkele lam word gebore.

Massa	.11 kg
Skouerhoogte	50 cm
Rekordhoringlengte	19 cm
Draagtyd	5,5 maande

**KRUGER/GOLDEN GATE/
BERGKWAGGA/
BONTEBOK/KAROO/
AUGRABIES/
KALAHARI-GEMSBOK/
LANGEBAAN**

STEENBOK *Raphicerus campestris*

Occurs in most of our national parks but absent from Addo and Tsitsikamma. Only the males have horns. They are active in the early part of the day and again in late afternoon. Usually a single lamb is born.

Mass	11 kg
Shoulder height	50 cm
Record horn length	19 cm
Gestation period	5,5 months

**KRUGER/GOLDEN GATE/
MOUNTAIN ZEBRA/
BONTEBOK/KAROO/
AUGRABIES/
KALAHARIGEMSBOK/
LANGEBAAN**

LE STEENBOK *Raphicerus campestris*

On le rencontre dans la plupart de nos parcs nationaux, à l'exception des parcs nationaux Addo et Tsitsikamma. Seuls les mâles sont pourvus de cornes. Les steenboks sont actifs tôt le matin et en fin d'après-midi. La femelle ne donne généralement naissance qu'à un jeune.

Poids	.11 kg
Hauteur au garrot	50 cm
Longueur record des cornes	19 cm
Durée de la gestation	5,5 mois

**KRUGER/GOLDEN GATE/
ZÈBRE DE MONTAGNE/
BONTEBOK/KAROO/
AUGRABIES/
KALAHARI GEMSBOK/
LANGEBAAN**

STEINBÖCKCHEN *Raphicerus campestris*

Das Tier kommt in den meisten unserer Nationalparks vor, aber nicht im Addo- und Tsitsikammapark. Nur die Männchen haben Hörner. Sie sind frühmorgens aktiv und dann wieder am späten Nachmittag. Gewöhnlich wird ein einziges Kitz geboren.

Gewicht	.11 kg
Schulterhöhe	50 cm
Rekordlänge der Hörner	19 cm
Trächtigkeitszeit	5,5 Monate

**KRUGER/GOLDEN GATE/
MOUNTAIN ZEBRA/
BONTEBOK/KAROO/
AUGRABIES/
KALAHARI GEMSBOK/
LANGEBAAN**

GRYSBOK *Raphicerus melanotis*

'n Baie skugter klein antiloop wat normaalweg slegs snags aktief is. 'n Enkele lam word gewoonlik in die lente gebore.

Massa	. . . . .10 kg
Skouerhoogte	. . . . 55 cm
Rekordhoringlengte	. . . . . 12 cm
Draagtyd	. . . . 6 maande

**ADDO/
TSITSIKAMMA/
BONTEBOK/
LANGEBAAN**

GRYSBOK *Raphicerus melanotis*

The grysbok is a shy and elusive antelope and is active normally only at night. A single lamb is born, usually in spring.

Mass	. . . . 10 kg
Shoulder height	. . . . 55 cm
Record horn length	. . . . 12 cm
Gestation period	. . . . . . 6 months

**ADDO/
TSITSIKAMMA/
BONTEBOK/
LANGEBAAN**

LE GRYSBOK *Raphicerus melanotis*

Le grysbok est un petit animal timide et farouche, normalement actif uniquement de nuit. La femelle met bas un seul jeune, d'habitude au printemps.

Poids	. . . . .10 kg
Hauteur au garrot	. . . . 55 cm
Longueur record des cornes	. . 12 cm
Durée de la gestation	. . . . . . 6 mois

**ADDO/
TSITSIKAMMA/
BONTEBOK/
LANGEBAAN**

GRAUBÖCKCHEN *Raphicerus melanotis*

Das Grauböckchen ist eine scheue, kleine Antilope, die normalerweise nur nachts aktiv ist. Ein einziges Kitz wird gewöhnlich im Frühling geboren.

Gewicht	. . . . .10 kg
Schulterhöhe	. . . . 55 cm
Rekordlänge der Hörner	. . . . 12 cm
Trächtigkeitszeit	. . . . . . 6 Monate

**ADDO/
TSITSIKAMMA/
BONTEBOK/
LANGEBAAN**

SHARPE-GRYSBOK *Raphicerus sharpei*

Word in die mopanieveld van veral die noordelike gedeelte van die Nasionale Krugerwildtuin aangetref. Gewoonlik wei dit snags, is baie skugter en word dus baie selde gesien. Die ooi (regs afgebeeld) het geen horings nie. 'n Enkele lam word per werpsel gebore.

Massa	7,5 kg
Skouerhoogte	45 cm
Rekordhoringlengte	10,5 cm
Draagtyd	6 maande

KRUGER

SHARPE'S GRYSBOK *Raphicerus sharpei*

This animal is found in the mopane veld of the northern part of the Kruger National Park. Generally feeds during the night and is very timid; for this reason it is seldom seen. Female (shown opposite) has no horns. A single lamb is born.

Mass	7,5 kg
Shoulder height	45 cm
Record horn length	10,5 cm
Gestation period	6 months

KRUGER

LE GRYSBOK DE SHARPE *Raphicerus sharpei*

On trouve cet animal dans les steppes de mopanies au nord du Parc National Kruger. Il se nourrit généralement la nuit et est extrêmement timide de nature; c'est pourquoi on le voit rarement. La femelle (illustration ci-contre) n'a pas de cornes. Elle met bas un seul jeune.

Poids	7,5 kg
Hauteur au garrot	45 cm
Longueur record des cornes	10,5 cm
Durée de la gestation	6 mois

KRUGER

SHARPE-GRAUBÖCKCHEN *Raphicerus sharpei*

Dieses Tier wird im Mopaneveld im nördlichen Teil des Kruger Nationalparks gefunden. Gewöhnlich sucht es nachts seine Nahrung. Es ist sehr scheu und wird deshalb selten gesehen. Das Weibchen (siehe Abbildung) hat keine Hörner. Ein einziges Kitz wird geboren.

Gewicht	7,5 kg
Schulterhöhe	45 cm
Rekordlänge der Hörner	10,5 cm
Trächtigkeitszeit	6 Monate

KRUGER

OORBIETJIE *Ourebia ourebi*

Hierdie elegante antiloop is ongelukkig besig om oor sy hele verspreidingsgebied uit te sterf. Dit verkies oop grasvelde met lang gras wat skuiling bied. 'n Enkele lam word gebore, gewoonlik in die somer.

Massa . . . . .14 kg
Skouerhoogte . . . . 60 cm
Rekordhoringlengte . . . . . 19 cm
Moontlike lewensduur . . . . 13,5 jaar
Draagtyd . . . . 7 maande

KRUGER/
GOLDEN GATE

ORIBI *Ourebia ourebi*

This graceful antelope is unfortunately declining over most of its range. It frequents open grasslands as long as there is long grass available for cover. One lamb is born, usually in summer.

Mass . . . . 14 kg
Shoulder height . . . . 60 cm
Record horn length . . . . . . 19 cm
Potential longevity . . . . . 13,5 years
Gestation period . . . . . . 7 months

KRUGER/
GOLDEN GATE

L'ORIBI *Ourebia ourebi*

Cette gracieuse antilope est malheureusement en voie d'extinction. Elle fréquente les savanes où l'herbe est assez haute pour l'abriter. Elle met bas un petit, généralement en été.

Poids . . . . .14 kg
Hauteur au garrot . . . . 60 cm
Longueur record des cornes . . 19 cm
Longévité . . . . 13,5 ans
Durée de la gestation . . . . . . 7 mois

KRUGER/
GOLDEN GATE

ORIBI *Ourebia ourebi*

Diese graziöse Antilope ist leider in den meisten Gebieten am Aussterben. Sie bevorzugt die Savanne und versteckt sich gerne im langen Gras. Im Sommer wird meistens ein einziges Kitz geboren.

Gewicht . . . . .14 kg
Schulterhöhe . . . . 60 cm
Rekordlänge der Hörner . . . . 19 cm
Mögliche Lebensdauer . . . 13,5 Jahre
Trächtigkeitszeit . . . . . . 7 Monate

KRUGER/
GOLDEN GATE

SOENIE *Neotragus moschatus*

Word in 'n beperkte omgewing in die noorde van die Nasionale Krugerwildtuin aangetref. Dit woon in digte ruigtes. 'n Enkele lam word gewoonlik in die somer gebore.

Massa . . . . 5 kg
Skouerhoogte . . . . 35 cm
Rekordhoringlengte . . . . . . 13 cm
Draagtyd . . . . 6 maande

KRUGER

SUNI *Neotragus moschatus*

Occurs in a limited area in the north of the Kruger National Park. It lives in dense thickets. A single lamb is born, usually in summer.

Mass . . . . 5 kg
Shoulder height . . . . 35 cm
Record horn length . . . . . . 13 cm
Gestation period . . . . . . 6 months

KRUGER

LE SUNI *Neotragus moschatus*

On le trouve dans une aire restreinte du Parc National Kruger, où il vit dans des fourrés denses. La femelle met bas un seul jeune, généralement en été.

Poids . . . . 5 kg
Hauteur au garrot . . . . 35 cm
Longueur record des cornes . . 13 cm
Durée de la gestation . . . . . 6 mois

KRUGER

SUNIBÖCKCHEN *Neotragus moschatus*

Das Tier kommt in einem kleinen Gebiet im Norden des Kruger Nationalparks vor. Es lebt in dichtem Busch. Ein einziges Kitz wird geboren, meistens im Sommer.

Gewicht . . . . 5 kg
Schulterhöhe . . . . 35 cm
Rekordlänge der Hörner . . . . 13 cm
Trächtigkeitszeit . . . . . . 6 Monate

KRUGER

KLIPSPRINGER *Oreotragus oreotragus*

Word op klipkoppies en in bergagtige gedeeltes van die
Nasionale Krugerwildtuin en die Bergkwagga, Karoo en
Augrabieswaterval nasionale parke aangetref. 'n Enkele
lam word gebore, maar daar is geen vaste paartyd nie.

Massa	.11 kg
Skouerhoogte	60 cm
Rekordhoringlengte	16 cm
Draagtyd	7 maande

**KRUGER/
BERGKWAGGA/
KAROO/
AUGRABIES**

KLIPSPRINGER *Oreotragus oreotragus*

Occurs in the hilly and mountainous areas of the Kruger,
Mountain Zebra, Karoo and Augrabies national parks. A
single lamb is born, but there is no fixed breeding season.

Mass (female)	11 kg
Shoulder height	60 cm
Record horn length	16 cm
Gestation period	7 months

**KRUGER/
MOUNTAIN ZEBRA/
KAROO/
AUGRABIES**

L'ANTILOPE SAUTEUSE *Oreotragus oreotragus*

On rencontre cette antilope dans les collines et les zones
montagneuses des parcs nationaux Kruger, Karoo,
Augrabies et Zèbre de Montagne. La femelle n'a qu'un petit
et il n'y a pas de saison de reproduction fixe.

Poids de la femelle	11 kg
Hauteur au garrot	60 cm
Longueur record des cornes	16 cm
Durée de la gestation	7 mois

**KRUGER/
ZÈBRE DE MONTAGNE/
KAROO/
AUGRABIES**

KLIPPSPRINGER *Oreotragus oreotragus*

Das Tier lebt in den hügeligen und gebirgigen Gegenden
der Kruger-, Karoo- und Augrabies Nationalparks. Ein
einziges Kitz wird geboren. Es gibt keine feste
Paarungszeit.

Gewicht (Weibchen)	11 kg
Schulterhöhe	60 cm
Rekordlänge der Hörner	16 cm
Trächtigkeitszeit	7 Monate

**KRUGER/
MOUNTAIN ZEBRA/
KAROO/
AUGRABIES**

VAALRIBBOK *Pelea capreolus*

Die vaalribbok vlug met 'n kenmerkende 'skommel-perdbeweging' en wys die wit onderkant van die stert. 'n Enkele lam word in November of Desember gebore. Slegs die ram het horings. Dit is onlangs in die Malelane-omgewing van die Nasionale Krugerwildtuin hervestig.

Massa	.20 kg
Skouerhoogte	75 cm
Rekordhoringlengte	29 cm
Draagtyd	8,5 maande

**KRUGER/
GOLDEN GATE/
BERGKWAGGA/
BONTEBOK/
KAROO**

GREY RHEBOK *Pelea capreolus*

When fleeing the grey rhebok has a characteristic 'rocking-horse' action, and shows the white underside of the tail. A single young is born in November or December. Only the male has horns. Recently reintroduced to the Malelane area of the Kruger National Park.

Mass	20 kg
Shoulder height	75 cm
Record horn length	29 cm
Gestation period	8,5 months

**KRUGER/
GOLDEN GATE/
MOUNTAIN ZEBRA/
BONTEBOK/
KAROO**

LE RHEBOK GRIS *Pelea capreolus*

Lorsqu'il s'enfuit, le rhebok gris ressemble à un cheval à bascule et on voit le dessous blanc de sa queue. Seul le mâle est pourvu de cornes. On l'a récemment réintroduit dans la région de Malelane (Parc National Kruger). Un seul petit nait en novembre ou en décembre.

Poids	.20 kg
Hauteur au garrot	75 cm
Longueur record des cornes	29 cm
Durée de la gestation	8,5 mois

**KRUGER/
GOLDEN GATE/
ZÈBRE DE MONTAGNE/
BONTEBOK/
KAROO**

REHBOCK *Pelea capreolus*

Wenn der Rehbock flieht, bewegt er sich wie ein Schaukelpferd und zeigt die untere Seite des Schwanzes. Ein einziges Junges wird im November oder Dezember geboren. Nur das Männchen hat Hörner. Vor kurzem wurde das Tier auch ins Malelanegebiet des Kruger Nationalparks eingeführt.

Gewicht	.20 kg
Schulterhöhe	75 cm
Rekordlänge der Hörner	29 cm
Trächtigkeitszeit	.8,5 Monate

**KRUGER/
GOLDEN GATE/
MOUNTAIN ZEBRA/
BONTEBOK/
KAROO**

ROOIRIBBOK *Redunca fulvorufula*

In die Nasionale Krugerwildtuin word dit veral in die heuwels noordwes van Malelane aangetref. Die antiloop kom ook voor in die Bergkwagga, Karoo en Golden Gate nasionale parke. 'n Enkele lam word gebore, gewoonlik in die somer.

Massa	.30 kg
Skouerhoogte	75 cm
Rekordhoringlengte	25 cm
Moontlike lewensduur	.8 jaar
Draagtyd	8 maande

**KRUGER/
GOLDEN GATE/
BERGKWAGGA/
KAROO**

MOUNTAIN REEDBUCK *Redunca fulvorufula*

In the Kruger National Park it is chiefly observed in the hills north-west of Malelane. This antelope is also found in the Mountain Zebra, Karoo and Golden Gate Highlands national parks. A single lamb is born, usually in summer.

Mass	30 kg
Shoulder height	75 cm
Record horn length	25 cm
Potential longevity	.8 years
Gestation period	8 months

**KRUGER/
GOLDEN GATE/
MOUNTAIN ZEBRA/
KAROO**

LE COB DES MONTAGNES *Redunca fulvorufula*

Dans le Parc National Kruger on le rencontre surtout dans les collines au nord-ouest de Malelane. Il habite également les parcs du Zèbre de Montagne, Karoo et Golden Gate. La mise-bas, d'un seul jeune, a généralement lieu en été.

Poids	.30 kg
Hauteur au garrot	75 cm
Longueur record des cornes	25 cm
Longévité	8 ans
Durée de la gestation	8 mois

**KRUGER/
GOLDEN GATE/
ZÈBRE DE MONTAGNE/
KAROO**

BERGRIEDBOCK *Redunca fulvorufula*

Das Tier wird im Kruger Nationalpark hauptsächlich in den Hügeln nordwestlich von Malelane beobachtet, kommt aber auch im Mountain Zebra-, Karoo- und Golden Gate Highlands Nationalpark vor. Ein einziges Kitz wird geboren, meistens im Sommer.

Gewicht	.30 kg
Schulterhöhe	75 cm
Rekordlänge der Hörner	25 cm
Mögliche Lebensdauer	.8 Jahre
Trächtigkeitszeit	8 Monate

**KRUGER/
GOLDEN GATE/
MOUNTAIN ZEBRA/
KAROO**

RIETBOK *Redunca arundinum*

Die rietbok kom voor in digbegroeide rietkolle en grasvleie naby riviere van die Nasionale Krugerwildtuin. As hy skrik, uiter hy 'n skerp fluitgeluid en hardloop weg met 'n kenmerkende 'skommelperdbeweging' - dit laat die wit onderkant van die stertkwas wys wat dien as 'n alarmteken. 'n Enkele lam word gewoonlik in die somer gebore.

Massa	.60 kg
Skouerhoogte	90 cm
Rekordhoringlengte	46 cm
Moontlike lewensduur	.9 jaar
Draagtyd	7,5 maande

**KRUGER/
GOLDEN GATE**

REEDBUCK *Redunca arundinum*

The reedbuck frequents thickly grown patches of reed and vleis near rivers of the Kruger National Park. It utters a sharp whistle when alarmed, and when fleeing has a rolling 'rocking-horse' gait, showing the white underside of the tail as an alarm signal. A single lamb is born, usually in summer.

Mass	60 kg
Shoulder height	90 cm
Record horn length	46 cm
Potential longevity	.9 years
Gestation period	.7,5 months

**KRUGER/
GOLDEN GATE**

LE COB DES ROSEAUX *Redunca arundinum*

Ce cob se plaît dans les fourrés de roseaux et dans les zones marécageuses du Parc National Kruger. Il émet un sifflement strident quand il prend peur. Lorsqu'il s'enfuit, il ressemble à un cheval à bascule et montre le dessous blanc de sa queue (ce qui constitue un signe d'alarme). La femelle met bas un seul petit, généralement en été.

Poids	.60 kg
Hauteur au garrot	90 cm
Longueur record des cornes	46 cm
Longévité	9 ans
Durée de la gestation	7,5 mois

**KRUGER/
GOLDEN GATE**

GROSSER RIEDBOCK *Redunca arundinum*

Der Riedbock ist in dichtem Schilf und sumpfigen Gegenden in der Nähe der Flüsse im Kruger Nationalpark zu Hause. Wenn er erschreckt wird, stößt er einen schrillen Pfiff aus. Auf der Flucht hat er eine Schaukelpferd-Gangart, und zeigt so die weiße Unterseite seines Schwanzes als Alarm- zeichen. Ein einziges Kitz wird gewöhnlich im Sommer geboren.

Gewicht	.60 kg
Schulterhöhe	90 cm
Rekordlänge der Hörner	46 cm
Mögliche Lebensdauer	.9 Jahre
Trächtigkeitszeit	7,5 Monate

**KRUGER/
GOLDEN GATE**

WATERBOK *Kobus ellipsiprymnus*

Die waterbok is betreklik volop in die Nasionale Krugerwildtuin. Die wit kring op die kruis om die stert is 'n opvallende kenmerk. Word veral naby water aangetref. 'n Enkele kalf word gebore, gewoonlik in Januarie of Februarie.

Massa	250 kg
Skouerhoogte (ram)	130 cm
Rekordhoringlengte	99 cm
Moontlike lewensduur	12 jaar
Draagtyd	9 maande

KRUGER

WATERBUCK *Kobus ellipsiprymnus*

The waterbuck is comparatively abundant in the Kruger National Park. A single calf is born, usually in January or February. The white circle on the rump around the tail is a conspicuous characteristic. It is especially abundant near water.

Mass	250 kg
Shoulder height (male)	130 cm
Record horn length	99 cm
Potential longevity	12 years
Gestation period	9 months

KRUGER

LE COB à CROISSANT *Kobus ellipsiprymnus*

Ce cob est assez répandu dans le Parc National Kruger. La femelle donne le jour à un seul jeune, généralement en janvier ou février. Cet animal est caractérisé par la présence d'un cercle blanc sur la croupe, autour de la queue. Il affectionne particulièrement le voisinage des points d'eau.

Poids	250 kg
Hauteur au garrot (mâle)	130 cm
Longueur record des cornes	99 cm
Longévité	12 ans
Durée de la gestation	9 mois

KRUGER

ELLIPSEN-WASSERBOCK *Kobus ellipsiprymnus*

Der Wasserbock kommt verhältnismäßig häufig im Kruger Nationalpark vor. Ein einziges Kalb wird gewöhnlich im Januar oder Februar geboren. Der weiße Kreis am Rumpf rund um den Schwanz ist ein auffallendes, charakteristisches Merkmal. Das Tier kommt meist in der Nähe von Wasser vor.

Gewicht	250 kg
Schulterhöhe (Männchen)	130 cm
Rekordlänge der Hörner	99 cm
Mögliche Lebensdauer	12 Jahre
Trächtigkeitszeit	9 Monate

KRUGER

ROOIBOK *Aepyceros melampus*

Die rooibok is die mees algemene boksoort in die Nasionale Krugerwildtuin en word veral suid van die Sabierivier in groot troppe aangetref. Dit kan tot 10 m ver en 3 m hoog spring. Die paringseisoen is April tot Mei en 'n enkele lam word gewoonlik in November of Desember gebore.

Massa	.50 kg
Skouerhoogte	90 cm
Rekordhoringlengte	81 cm
Draagtyd	6,5 maande

KRUGER

IMPALA *Aepyceros melampus*

The impala is the most common antelope in the Kruger National Park and is found in large herds particularly south of the Sabie River. It can leap a distance of 10 m and clear a height of 3 m. The mating season is April to May and a single lamb is born, usually in November or December.

Mass	50 kg
Shoulder height	90 cm
Record horn length	81 cm
Gestation period	.6,5 months

KRUGER

L'IMPALA *Aepyceros melampus*

L'impala est l'antilope la plus commune du Parc National Kruger et on la rencontre en grands troupeaux, particulièrement près de la rivière Sabie. Cet animal peut effectuer des bonds de 10 m de long et 3 m de haut. La saison de reproduction se situe en avril et en mai et il y a un seul petit par portée, qui nait généralement en novembre ou décembre.

Poids	.50 kg
Hauteur au garrot	90 cm
Longueur record des cornes	81 cm
Durée de la gestation	6,5 mois

KRUGER

IMPALA *Aepyceros melampus*

Der Impala ist die Antilope, die im Kruger Nationalpark am häufigsten vorkommt. Er ist in großen Rudeln besonders südlich des Sabieflusses zu finden. Er kann 10 m weit und 3 m hoch springen. Die Paarungszeit ist im April und Mai. Ein einziges Kitz wird gewöhnlich im November oder Dezember geboren.

Gewicht	.50 kg
Schulterhöhe	90 cm
Rekordlänge der Hörner	81 cm
Trächtigkeitszeit	.6,5 Monate

KRUGER

SPRINGBOK *Antidorcas marsupialis*

Die springbok kom voor in al die droër, westelike nasionale parke behalwe die Nasionale Krugerwildtuin. 'n Enkele lam word gewoonlik in November gedurende die somerreënvalseisoen gebore.

Massa	.40 kg
Skouerhoogte	75 cm
Rekordhoringlengte	49 cm
Moontlike lewensduur	10 jaar
Draagtyd	5,5 maande

**GOLDEN GATE/
BERGKWAGGA/
KAROO/
AUGRABIES/
KALAHARI-GEMSBOK**

SPRINGBOK *Antidorcas marsupialis*

The springbok is found in all the drier western national parks but is absent from the Kruger National Park. A single lamb is born, usually during November in the summer-rainfall areas.

Mass	40 kg
Shoulder height	75 cm
Record horn length	49 cm
Potential longevity	10 years
Gestation period	5,5 months

**GOLDEN GATE/
MOUNTAIN ZEBRA/
KAROO/
AUGRABIES/
KALAHARI GEMSBOK**

LE SPRINGBOK *Antidorcas marsupialis*

Le springbok vit dans tous les parcs nationaux à l'exception du Parc National Kruger. La femelle met bas un seul petit, généralement en novembre dans la zone des pluies d'été.

Poids	.40 kg
Hauteur au garrot	75 cm
Longueur record des cornes	49 cm
Longévité	10 ans
Durée de la gestation	5,5 mois

**GOLDEN GATE/
ZÈBRE DE MONTAGNE/
KAROO/
AUGRABIES/
KALAHARI GEMSBOK**

SPRINGBOCK *Antidorcas marsupialis*

Der Springbock kommt in allen trocknen Nationalparks im Westen des Landes vor, aber nicht im Kruger Nationalpark. Ein einziges Kitz wird geboren, gewöhnlich im November in den Gebieten mit Sommerregen.

Gewicht	.40 kg
Schulterhöhe	75 cm
Rekordlänge der Hörner	49 cm
Mögliche Lebensdauer	10 Jahre
Trächtigkeitszeit	5,5 Monate

**GOLDEN GATE/
MOUNTAIN ZEBRA/
KAROO/
AUGRABIES/
KALAHARI GEMSBOK**

GEMSBOK *Oryx gazella*

Bewoner van die dorre, waterlose geweste en is veral baie volop in die woestynagtige Kalahari-gemsbok Nasionale Park waar hulle soms vir maande aaneen sonder water kan klaarkom. 'n Enkele kalf word enige tyd van die jaar gebore.

Massa	225 kg
Skouerhoogte	120 cm
Rekordhoringlengte	122 cm
Moontlike lewensduur	19 jaar
Draagtyd	9 maande

**KAROO/
AUGRABIES/
KALAHARI-GEMSBOK**

GEMSBOK *Oryx gazella*

Inhabits the waterless regions of the country, and is particularly numerous in the semi-desert Kalahari Gemsbok National Park. It can survive without water for months on end. A single calf is born at anytime of the year.

Mass	225 kg
Shoulder height	120 cm
Record horn length	122 cm
Potential longevity	19 years
Gestation period	9 months

**KAROO/
AUGRABIES/
KALAHARI GEMSBOK**

LE GEMSBOK *Oryx gazella*

Cet oryx habite les zones arides du pays et est particulièrement répandu dans le Parc National du Kalahari Gemsbok (semi-desert). Il peut survivre sans eau pendant des mois d'affilée. La femelle n'a qu'un petit, à n'importe quelle période de l'année.

Poids	225 kg
Hauteur au garrot	120 cm
Longueur record des cornes	122 cm
Longévité	19 ans
Durée de la gestation	9 mois

**KAROO/
AUGRABIES/
KALAHARI GEMSBOK**

SÜDAFRIKANISCHER SPIESSBOCK *Oryx gazella*

Der Südafrikanischer Spießbock bewohnt die wasserlosen Gegenden des Landes und ist besonders zahlreich im Kalahari Gemsbok Nationalpark, einer Halbwüste. Er kann viele Monate ohne Wasser leben. Ein einziges Kalb kann zu irgendeiner Jahreszeit geboren werden.

Gewicht	225 kg
Schulterhöhe	120 cm
Rekordlänge der Hörner	122 cm
Mögliche Lebensdauer	19 Jahre
Trächtigkeitszeit	9 Monate

**KAROO/
AUGRABIES/
KALAHARI GEMSBOK**

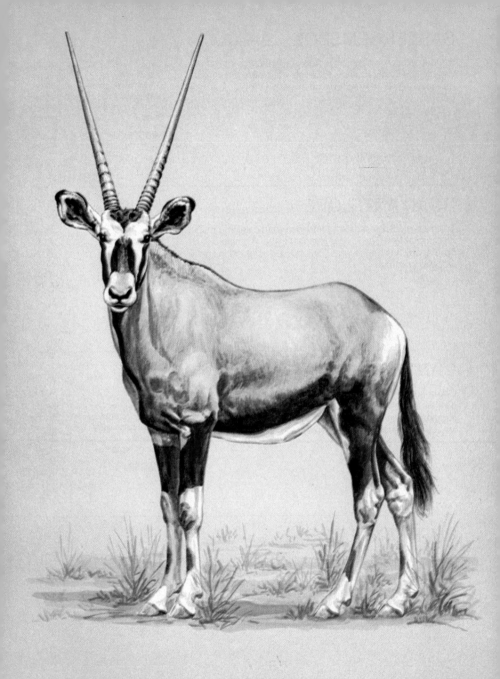

BASTERGEMSBOK *Hippotragus equinus*

Hierdie seldsame boksoort word veral in die noordelike dele van die Nasionale Krugerwildtuin op ylbeboste grasvlaktes aangetref. 'n Enkele kalfie word enige tyd van die jaar gebore.

Massa	270 kg
Skouerhoogte	140 cm
Rekordhoringlengte	99 cm
Lengte van oor	26 cm
Moontlike lewensduur	19 jaar
Draagtyd	9 maande

KRUGER

ROAN ANTELOPE *Hippotragus equinus*

This rare antelope has its haunts more particularly in the northern parts of the Kruger National Park. A single calf is born at any time of the year. The species is found in lightly wooded savanna.

Mass	270 kg
Shoulder height	140 cm
Record horn length	99 cm
Length of ear	26 cm
Potential longevity	19 years
Gestation period	9 months

KRUGER

L'ANTILOPE ROUANE *Hippotragus equinus*

On rencontre cette rare antilope principalement dans le nord du Parc National Kruger. La femelle met bas un seul petit, à n'importe quelle période de l'année. Cette espèce peuple les savanes quelque peu arborées.

Poids	270 kg
Hauteur au garrot	140 cm
Longueur record des cornes	99 cm
Longueur des oreilles	26 cm
Longévité	19 ans
Durée de la gestation	9 mois

KRUGER

PFERDANTILOPE *Hippotragus equinus*

Dieses seltene Tier hat seine Aufenthaltsorte vor allem im nördlichen Teil des Kruger Nationalparks. Ein einziges Kalb wird zu irgendeiner Jahreszeit geboren. Die Pferdantilope wird in der leicht bebuschten Savanne angetroffen.

Gewicht	270 kg
Schulterhöhe	140 cm
Rekordlänge der Hörner	99 cm
Länge des Ohres	26 cm
Mögliche Lebensdauer	19 Jahre
Trächtigkeitszeit	9 Monate

KRUGER

SWARTWITPENS *Hippotragus niger*

Kom voor in die meeste dele van die Nasionale
Krugerwildtuin, maar verkies ylbeboste grasvlaktes. 'n
Enkele kalfie word gebore, gewoonlik gedurende Januarie
tot Maart.

Massa	230 kg
Skouerhoogte	135 cm
Rekordhoringlengte	154 cm
Lengte van ore	20 cm
Moontlike lewensduur	19 jaar
Draagtyd	9 maande

KRUGER

SABLE ANTELOPE *Hippotragus niger*

Sable prefer savanna woodland habitats and are present in
most parts of the Kruger National Park. The lambing
season is usually from January to March and a single calf is
born.

Mass	230 kg
Shoulder height	135 cm
Record horn length	154 cm
Length of ears	20 cm
Potential longevity	19 years
Gestation period	9 months

KRUGER

L'HIPPOTRAGUE NOIR *Hippotragus niger*

Ces antilopes vivent dans la plupart des zones du Parc
National Kruger et sont particulièrement répandues dans les
savanes arborées. La mise-bas, d'un seul jeune, a
généralement lieu entre janvier et mars.

Poids	230 kg
Hauteur au garrot	135 cm
Longueur record des cornes	154 cm
Longueur des oreilles	20 cm
Longévité	19 ans
Durée de la gestation	9 mois

KRUGER

RAPPENANTILOPE *Hippotragus niger*

Die Rappenantilope bevorzugt die bebuschte Savanne und
wird fast überall im Kruger Nationalpark angetroffen. Die
Setzzeit ist gewöhnlich von Januar bis März und ein
einziges Kalb wird geboren.

Gewicht	230 kg
Schulterhöhe	135 cm
Rekordlänge der Hörner	154 cm
Länge der Ohren	20 cm
Mögliche Lebensdauer	19 Jahre
Trächtigkeitszeit	9 Monate

KRUGER ·

TSESSEBE *Damaliscus lunatus*

Kom voor in die noordelike deel van die Nasionale Krugerwildtuin. Dit maak hoofsaaklik staat op sy spoed en ratsheid om groot roofdiere te ontvlug. 'n Enkele kalf word gebore, gewoonlik in September of Oktober.

Massa	140 kg
Skouerhoogte	120 cm
Rekordhoringlengte	47 cm
Moontlike lewensduur	20 jaar
Draagtyd	8 maande

KRUGER

TSESSEBE *Damaliscus lunatus*

More plentiful in the northern section of the Kruger National Park. This animal relies mainly on its speed and agility to escape large predators. A single calf is born, usually during September or October.

Mass	140 kg
Shoulder height	120 cm
Record horn length	47 cm
Potential longevity	20 years
Gestation period	8 months

KRUGER

LE SASSABY *Damaliscus lunatus*

Ces damalisques sont très répandues dans le nord du Parc National Kruger. Leur aptitude à la course et leur agilité constituent pratiquement leurs seuls moyens de défense face aux gros prédateurs. La femelle n'a qu'un petit, qui naît généralement en septembre ou en octobre.

Poids	140 kg
Hauteur au garrot	120 cm
Longueur record des cornes	47 cm
Longévité	20 ans
Durée de la gestation	8 mois

KRUGER

HALBMONDANTILOPE *Damaliscus lunatus*

Dieses Tier kommt häufig im nördlichen Teil des Kruger Nationalparks vor. Es verläßt sich hauptsächlich auf seine Schnelligkeit und Behendigkeit, um den großen Raubtieren zu entfliehen. Ein einziges Kalb wird im September oder Oktober geboren.

Gewicht	140 kg
Schulterhöhe	120 cm
Rekordlänge der Hörner	47 cm
Mögliche Lebensdauer	20 Jahre
Trächtigkeitszeit	8 Monate

KRUGER

BONTEBOK *Damaliscus dorcas dorcas*

Die bontebok is inheems in 'n beperkte gebied van suid-westelike Kaapland. Een van die grootste troppe word in die Bontebokpark by Swellendam gevind. Die wit bles oor die gesig is ononderbroke en die kruis, bene en pens is wit (kyk blesbok).

Massa (ram)	.60 kg
Skouerhoogte	90 cm
Rekordhoringlengte	43 cm
Draagtyd	8 maande

BONTEBOK/ LANGEBAAN

BONTEBOK *Damaliscus dorcas dorcas*

The bontebok is native to a restricted area of the south-west Cape. One of the largest herds is found in the Bontebok National Park at Swellendam where it was protected after its near-extinction. The white facial blaze is undivided and the rump, legs and belly are white (see blesbok).

Mass (male)	.60 kg
Shoulder height	90 cm
Record horn length	43 cm
Gestation period	8 months

BONTEBOK/ LANGEBAAN

LE BONTEBOK *Damaliscus dorcas dorcas*

Le bontebok est originaire d'une petite zone du sud-ouest de la province du Cap. Un des plus grands troupeaux se trouve dans le Park National Bontebok (à Swellendam), où l'animal a été mis dans une réserve alors qu'il était en voie d'extinction. La marque blanche sur son visage est pleine et la croupe, les pattes et le ventre sont blancs.

Poids du mâle	60 kg
Hauteur au garrot	90 cm
Longueur record des cornes	43 cm
Durée de la gestation	8 mois

BONTEBOK/ LANGEBAAN

BUNTBOCK *Damaliscus dorcas dorcas*

Der Buntbock ist in einem kleinen Gebiet der südwestlichen Kapprovinz heimisch. Eins der größten Rudel befindet sich im Bontebok Nationalpark, der bei Swellendam gelegen ist. Dort wurde das Tier geschützt, als es vom Aussterben bedroht war. Die Blesse am Kopf ist nicht unterteilt, und das Kreuz, die Beine und der Unterleib sind weiß (siehe Bleßbock).

Gewicht (Männchen)	60 kg
Schulterhöhe	90 cm
Rekordlänge der Hörner	43 cm
Trächtigkeitszeit	.8 Monate

BONTEBOK/ LANGEBAAN

BLESBOK *Damaliscus dorcas phillipsi*

'n Hoëveldse antiloop wat vanaf die Oos-Kaap tot in die Transvaal voorkom. Die wit bles op die voorkop is in twee verdeel (kyk bontebok). Die bene, pens en kruis is ligter van kleur as die res van die liggaam, maar nie so wit soos die bontebok nie.

Massa (ram)	.70 kg
Skouerhoogte	95 cm
Rekordhoringlengte	51 cm
Draagtyd	8 maande

**GOLDEN GATE/
BERGKWAGGA/
KAROO**

BLESBOK *Damaliscus dorcas phillipsi*

A highveld antelope occurring from the eastern Cape to the Transvaal. The white blaze on the forehead is divided into two between the eyes (see bontebok). The legs, belly and rump are lighter in colour than the rest of the body, but not as white as bontebok.

Mass (male)	.70 kg
Shoulder height	95 cm
Record horn length	51 cm
Gestation period	8 months

**GOLDEN GATE/
MOUNTAIN ZEBRA/
KAROO**

LE BLESBOK *Damaliscus dorcas phillipsi*

L'aire de répartition de cette antilope du haut veld va de l'est de la province du Cap jusqu'au Transvaal. La marque blanche sur le front est divisée en deux entre les yeux. Les pattes, le ventre et la croupe sont plus clairs que le reste du corps, mais pas aussi blancs que chez le bontebok.

Poids du mâle	70 kg
Hauteur au garrot	.95 kg
Longueur record des cornes	51 cm
Durée de la gestation	8 mois

**GOLDEN GATE/
ZÈBRE DE MONTAGNE/
KAROO**

BLESSBOCK *Damaliscus dorcas phillipsi*

Der Bleßbock ist eine Hochveld-Antilope, die vom Ostkap bis zum Transvaal vorkommt. Die Blesse auf der Stirn ist zwischen den Augen in zwei geteilt (siehe Buntbock). Die Läufe, der Unterleib und das Kreuz haben eine lichtere Farbe als der übrige Teil des Körpers, sind aber nicht so weiß wie beim Buntbock.

Gewicht (Männchen)	70 kg
Schulterhöhe	95 cm
Rekordlänge der Hörner	51 cm
Trächtigkeitszeit	.8 Monate

**GOLDEN GATE/
MOUNTAIN ZEBRA/
KAROO**

ROOIHARTBEES *Alcelaphus buselaphus*

Verkies vlaktewêreld of ylbeboste veld. Dit is 'n kuddedier en groot troppe kom dikwels vanaf Botswana in die Kalahari-gemsbok Nasionale Park in op soek na weiding. 'n Enkele kalfie word gebore, gewoonlik tussen September en Desember.

Massa (ram)	150 kg
Skouerhoogte	125 cm
Snelheid	65 km/h
Rekordhoringlengte	70 cm
Draagtyd	8 maande

**GOLDEN GATE/
BERGKWAGGA/
ADDO/KAROO/
AUGRABIES/
KALAHARI-GEMSBOK**

RED HARTEBEEST *Alcelaphus buselaphus*

Prefers the flat country of the plains or regions with sparse bush. A single calf is born, usually between September and December. It is a gregarious species and large herds often enter the Kalahari Gemsbok National Park from Botswana in search of grazing.

Mass (male)	150 kg
Shoulder height	125 cm
Speed	65 km/h
Record horn length	70 cm
Gestation period	8 months

**GOLDEN GATE/
MOUNTAIN ZEBRA/
ADDO/KAROO/
AUGRABIES/
KALAHARI GEMSBOK**

LE BUBALE ROUGE *Alcelaphus buselaphus*

Il préfère les regions plates ou celles où les buissons sont peu nombreux. C'est une espèce grégaire et de larges troupeaux en provenance du Botswana viennent souvent chercher des pâturages dans le Parc National Kalahari Gemsbok. La mise-bas, d'un seul jeune, a généralement lieu de septembre à décembre.

Poids du mâle	150 kg
Hauteur au garrot	125 cm
Vitesse	65 km/h
Longueur record des cornes	70 cm
Durée de la gestation	8 mois

**GOLDEN GATE/
ZÈBRE DE MONTAGNE/
ADDO/KAROO/
AUGRABIES/
KALAHARI GEMSBOK**

KUHANTILOPE *Alcelaphus buselaphus*

Dieses Tier zieht die Ebenen oder Gegenden mit nur lichtem Busch vor. Es ist ein Herdentier, und große Herden ziehen oft aus Botswana in den Kalahari Gemsbok Nationalpark auf der Suche nach Weide. Ein einziges Kalb wird zwischen September und Dezember geboren.

Gewicht (Männchen)	150 kg
Schulterhöhe	125 cm
Schnelligkeit	65 km/h
Rekordlänge der Hörner	70 cm
Trächtigkeitszeit	8 Monate

**GOLDEN GATE/
MOUNTAIN ZEBRA/
ADDO/KAROO/
AUGRABIES/
KALAHARI GEMSBOK**

BLOUWILDEBEES *Connochaetes taurinus*

Hierdie kuddedier versamel soms in groot troppe van 'n paar duisend. Die blouwildebees is bekend vir sy jaarlikse migrasies. 'n Enkele kalfie word gebore, gewoonlik tussen Desember en Januarie.

Massa (bul)	250 kg
Skouerhoogte (bul)	150 cm
Rekordhoringwydte	83 cm
Moontlike lewensduur	20 jaar
Draagtyd	8,5 maande

**KRUGER/
KALAHARI-GEMSBOK**

BLUE WILDEBEEST *Connochaetes taurinus*

This gregarious species sometimes forms large herds of several thousand individuals. It is well known for its annual migrations. A single calf is born, usually between December and January.

Mass (male)	250 kg
Shoulder height (male)	150 cm
Record span of horns	83 cm
Potential longevity	20 years
Gestation period	8,5 months

**KRUGER/
KALAHARI GEMSBOK**

LE GORGON BLEU *Connochaetes taurinus*

Cette espèce grégaire forme parfois d'immenses troupeaux de plusieurs milliers d'individus. Les gorgons sont bien connus pour leurs migrations annuelles. La femelle met bas un seul petit, généralement en décembre ou en janvier.

Poids du mâle	250 kg
Hauteur au garrot (mâle)	150 cm
Écartement record des cornes	83 cm
Longévité	20 ans
Durée de la gestation	8,5 mois

**KRUGER/
KALAHARI GEMSBOK**

STREIFENGNU *Connochaetes taurinus*

Das Streifengnu ist ein Wander- und Herdentier, das manchmal Herden von über tausend Tieren bildet. Ein einziges Kalb wird gewöhnlich im Dezember oder Januar geboren.

Gewicht (Männchen)	250 kg
Schulterhöhe (Männchen)	150 cm
Rekordspannweite der Hörner	83 cm
Mögliche Lebensdauer	20 Jahre
Trächtigkeitszeit	8,5 Monate

**KRUGER/
KALAHARI GEMSBOK**

SWARTWILDEBEES *Connochaetes gnou*

'n Hoëveldse kuddedier wat in die Bergkwagga, Golden Gate-Hoogland en Karoo nasionale parke voorkom. 'n Enkele kalfie word gebore, gewoonlik in Desember en Januarie.

Massa (bul)	180 kg
Skouerhoogte (bul)	120 cm
Rekordhoringlengte	70 cm
Moontlike lewensduur	20 jaar
Draagtyd	8,5 maande

**GOLDEN GATE/
BERGKWAGGA/
KAROO**

BLACK WILDEBEEST *Connochaetes gnou*

A highveld antelope which occurs in the Mountain Zebra, Golden Gate Highlands and Karoo national parks. A single calf is born, usually in December and January. It is gregarious by nature.

Mass (male)	180 kg
Shoulder height (male)	120 cm
Record horn length	70 cm
Potential longevity	20 years
Gestation period	8,5 months

**GOLDEN GATE/
MOUNTAIN ZEBRA/
KAROO**

LE GNOU NOIR *Connochaetes gnou*

On rencontre cette antilope du haut veld dans les parcs du Zèbre de Montagne, Golden Gate et Karoo. C'est un animal grégaire. La femelle n'a qu'un petit par portée, qui naît d'habitude en décembre ou en janvier.

Poids du mâle	180 kg
Hauteur au garrot (mâle)	120 cm
Longueur record des cornes	70 cm
Longévité	20 ans
Durée de la gestation	8,5 mois

**GOLDEN GATE/
ZÈBRE DE MONTAGNE/
KAROO**

WEISS-SCHWANZGNU *Connochaetes gnou*

Eine Hochveld-Antilope, die im Mountain Zebra-, Golden Gate- und Karoo Nationalpark in Herden vorkommt. Ein einziges Kalb wird meistens in Dezember oder Januar geboren.

Gewicht (Männchen)	180 kg
Schulterhöhe (Männchen)	120 cm
Rekordlänge der Hörner	70 cm
Mögliche Lebensdauer	20 Jahre
Trächtigkeitszeit	8,5 Monate

**GOLDEN GATE/
MOUNTAIN ZEBRA/
KAROO**

BOSBOK *Tragelaphus scriptus*

Alhoewel dit wydverspreid in die Nasionale Krugerwildtuin voorkom, word dit nie dikwels gesien nie aangesien dit die digte bosse en rietruigtes langs riviere verkies. Dit kom ook in die Tsitsikamma, Addo-olifant en Bergkwagga nasionale parke voor. 'n Enkele lam word gebore, gewoonlik in die lente of somer.

Massa (ram)	45 kg
Skouerhoogte (ram)	80 cm
Rekordhoringlengte	52 cm
Moontlike lewensduur	9 jaar
Draagtyd	6 maande

**KRUGER/
BERGKWAGGA/
ADDO/
TSITSIKAMMA**

BUSHBUCK *Tragelaphus scriptus*

Although widely distributed in the Kruger National Park the bushbuck is rarely seen as it frequents the dense bush and reeds along rivers. It also occurs in the Tsitsikamma, Addo Elephant and Mountain Zebra national parks. A single lamb is born, usually in spring or summer.

Mass (male)	45 kg
Shoulder height (male)	80 cm
Record horn length	52 cm
Potential longevity	9 years
Gestation period	6 months

**KRUGER/
MOUNTAIN ZEBRA/
ADDO/
TSITSIKAMMA**

LE GUIB HARNACHÉ *Tragelaphus scriptus*

Bien qu'il soit très répandu dans le Parc National Kruger, le guib harnaché est rarement visible car il habite des zones à forte concentration d'arbustes et de roseaux (le long des cours d'eau). On le rencontre également dans les parcs nationaux du Tsitsikamma, Addo et Zèbre de Montagne. La femelle ne met bas qu'un petit, généralement au printemps ou en été.

Poids du mâle	45 kg
Hauteur au garrot (mâle)	80 cm
Longueur record des cornes	52 cm
Longévité	9 ans
Durée de la gestation	6 mois

**KRUGER/
ZÈBRE DE MONTAGNE/
ADDO/
TSITSIKAMMA**

SCHIRRANTILOPE oder BUSCHBOCK *Tragelaphus scriptus*

Obgleich der Buschbock fast überall im Kruger Nationalpark vorkommt, wird er nur selten gesehen, da er meist im dichten Busch und im Schilf an den Flüssen seinen Einstand hat. Er hält sich auch im Tsitsikamma-, Mountain Zebra- und Addo Elephant Nationalpark auf. Nur ein Kitz wird meistens im Frühling oder im Sommer geboren.

Gewicht (Männchen)	45 kg
Schulterhöhe (Männchen)	80 cm
Rekordlänge der Hörner	52 cm
Mögliche Lebensdauer	9 Jahre
Trächtigkeitszeit	6 Monate

**KRUGER/
MOUNTAIN ZEBRA/
ADDO/
TSITSIKAMMA**

NJALA *Tragelaphus angasii*

Die njala se geliefkoosde boerplekke in die Nasionale Krugerwildtuin is langs die Luvuvhu- en Shingwedzi-riviere. Besonder talryk in die Pafuri-gebied. 'n Enkele lam word gebore, dikwels in die somer maar soms in die winter. Dit verkies redelik digte woude.

Massa (ram)	110 kg
Skouerhoogte (ram)	112 cm
Rekordhoringlengte	83 cm
Moontlike lewensduur	8 jaar
Draagtyd	7 maande

KRUGER

NYALA *Tragelaphus angasii*

The nyala's favourite haunts in the Kruger National Park are along the Luvuvhu and Shingwedzi rivers. Abundant in the Pafuri area. A single calf is born, often in summer but occasionally in winter. It prefers fairly dense woodland.

Mass (male)	110 kg
Shoulder height (male)	112 cm
Record horn length	83 cm
Potential longevity	8 years
Gestation period	7 months

KRUGER

LE NYALA *Tragelaphus angasii*

On rencontre le nyala surtout le long des rivières Luvuvhu et Shingwedzi dans le Parc National Kruger. Il est très répandu dans la région de Pafuri. Il affectionne les régions arborées. La femelle met bas un seul jeune, souvent en été mais parfois en hiver.

Poids du mâle	110 kg
Hauteur au garrot (mâle)	112 cm
Longueur record des cornes	83 cm
Longévité	8 ans
Durée de la gestation	7 mois

KRUGER

NYALA *Tragelaphus angasii*

Die Lieblingseinstände des Nyala im Kruger Nationalpark sind längs der Luvuvhu und Shingwedzi Flüsse. Sehr zahlreich kommt es in der Pafuri-gegend vor. Ein einziges Kalb wird geboren, meistens im Sommer, aber auch manchmal im Winter. Es bevorzugt ziemlich dichte Baumsteppen.

Gewicht (Männchen)	110 kg
Schulterhöhe (Männchen)	112 cm
Rekordlänge der Hörner	83 cm
Mögliche Lebensdauer	8 Jahre
Trächtigkeitszeit	7 Monate

KRUGER

KOEDOE *Tragelaphus strepsiceros*

Die koedoe is volop in die hele Nasionale Krugerwildtuin en word ook aangetref in talle ander parke. 'n Enkele kalf word gebore, gewoonlik in Maart en April, maar ook gedurende die res van die jaar.

Massa (bul)	250 kg
Skouerhoogte (bul)	140 cm
Rekordhoringlengte	181 cm
Moontlike lewensduur	11 jaar
Draagtyd	7 maande

**KRUGER/
BERGKWAGGA/
ADDO/KAROO/
AUGRABIES/
KALAHARI-GEMSBOK**

KUDU *Tragelaphus strepsiceros*

The kudu is well represented throughout the Kruger National Park and is also present in several other parks. A single calf is born, usually in March or April but also in other months of the year. It occurs in a variety of habitats but prefers broken country with thickets for cover.

Mass (male)	250 kg
Shoulder height (male)	140 cm
Record horn length	181 cm
Potential longevity	11 years
Gestation period	7 months

**KRUGER/
MOUNTAIN ZEBRA/
ADDO/KAROO/
AUGRABIES/
KALAHARI GEMSBOK**

LE KOUDOU *Tragelaphus strepsiceros*

Le koudou est très répandu dans l'ensemble du Parc National Kruger et est aussi présent dans plusieurs autres parcs. Il vit dans divers terrains mais préfère les zones accidentées et arbustives où il peut se mettre à couvert. La femelle met bas un seul petit, généralement en mars ou en avril, mais parfois aussi pendant le reste de l'année.

Poids du mâle	250 kg
Hauteur au garrot (mâle)	140 cm
Longueur record des cornes	181 cm
Longévité	11 ans
Durée de la gestation	7 mois

**KRUGER/
ZÈBRE DE MONTAGNE/
ADDO/KAROO/
AUGRABIES/
KALAHARI GEMSBOK**

GROSSER KUDU *Tragelaphus strepsiceros*

Der Kudu kommt häufig im Kruger Nationalpark, aber auch in einigen anderen Parks vor. Er ist in unterschiedlichen Umgebungen anzutreffen, meistens aber im buschigen Hügelland, wo er Unterschlupf findet. Ein einziges Kalb wird meistens im März oder April aber auch in anderen Monaten geboren.

Gewicht (Männchen)	250 kg
Schulterhöhe (Männchen)	140 cm
Rekordlänge der Hörner	181 cm
Mögliche Lebensdauer	11 Jahre
Trächtigkeitszeit	7 Monate

**KRUGER/
MOUNTAIN ZEBRA/
ADDO/KAROO/
AUGRABIES/
KALAHARI GEMSBOK**

ELAND *Taurotragus oryx*

In die Nasionale Krugerwildtuin word die eland van Letaba af noordwaarts aangetref. Dit kom ook in talle ander nasionale parke voor en kan in 'n groot verskeidenheid habitats oorleef. 'n Enkele kalf kan enige tyd van die jaar gebore word.

Massa (bul)	700 kg
Skouerhoogte (bul)	170 cm
Rekordhoringlengte	102 cm
Moontlike lewensduur	12 jaar
Draagtyd	9 maande

**KRUGER/GOLDEN GATE/
BERGKWAGGA/
ADDO/
KALAHARI-GEMSBOK/
LANGEBAAN**

ELAND *Taurotragus oryx*

In the Kruger National Park, the usual haunts of the eland are the northern districts, *i.e.* from Letaba northwards. It occurs in several other national parks and can flourish in a wide variety of habitats. The single calf can be born in any month of the year.

Mass (male)	700 kg
Shoulder height (male)	170 cm
Record horn length	102 cm
Potential longevity	12 years
Gestation period	9 months

**KRUGER/GOLDEN GATE/
MOUNTAIN ZEBRA/
ADDO/
KALAHARI GEMSBOK/
LANGEBAAN**

L'ÉLAND DU CAP *Taurotragus oryx*

On rencontre l'éland surtout dans le nord du Parc National Kruger, à partir du Letaba. On le trouve également dans plusieurs autres parcs nationaux et il s'épanouit dans de nombreux types d'habitats. L'unique petit est susceptible de naître à n'importe quelle période de l'année.

Poids du mâle	700 kg
Hauteur au garrot (mâle)	170 cm
Longueur record des cornes	102 cm
Longévité	12 ans
Durée de la gestation	9 mois

**KRUGER/GOLDEN GATE/
ZÈBRE DE MONTAGNE/
ADDO/
KALAHARI GEMSBOK/
LANGEBAAN**

ELENANTILOPE *Taurotragus oryx*

Der übliche Einstand der Elenantilope ist in den nördlichen Gebieten des Kruger Nationalparks, d.h. nördlich von Letaba. Sie kommt in einigen anderen Nationalparks vor und kann in vielen verschiedenen Umgebungen leben. Ein einziges Kalb kann zu irgendeiner Jahreszeit geboren werden.

Gewicht (Männchen)	700 kg
Schulterhöhe (Männchen)	170 cm
Rekordlänge der Hörner	102 cm
Mögliche Lebensdauer	12 Jahre
Trächtigkeitszeit	9 Monate

**KRUGER/GOLDEN GATE/
MOUNTAIN ZEBRA/
ADDO/
KALAHARI GEMSBOK/
LANGEBAAN**

BUFFEL *Syncerus caffer*

Die buffel kom in groot dele van die Nasionale Krugerwildtuin voor en is veral volop tussen Krokodilbrug en Onder-Sabie, in die sentrale distrik en noord van die Olifantsrivier. 'n Groot trop word ook in die Addo-olifant Nasionale Park beskerm - die enigste oorblywende buffels van die Suid-Kaapse stapel. 'n Enkele kalfie word gewoonlik tussen Januarie en April in die Nasionale Krugerwildtuin gebore.

Massa (bul)	800 kg
Skouerhoogte (bul)	140 cm
Snelheid oor 'n kort afstand	50 km/h
Rekordhoringspan	125 cm
Moontlike lewensduur	25 jaar
Draagtyd	11 maande

**KRUGER/
ADDO**

BUFFALO *Syncerus caffer*

The buffalo is present in large areas of the Kruger National Park and is particularly abundant in the area between Lower Sabie and Crocodile Bridge, in the central area and north of the Olifants River. A large herd is also protected in the Addo Elephant National Park - the only survivors of the southern Cape stock. A single calf is born, in the Kruger National Park usually between January and April.

Mass (male)	800 kg
Shoulder height	140 cm
Speed (short distance)	50 km/h
Record horn length	125 cm
Potential longevity	25 years
Gestation period	11 months

**KRUGER/
ADDO**

LE BUFFLE *Syncerus caffer*

On rencontre le buffle dans de larges régions du Parc National Kruger et particulièrement dans la région entre Lower Sabie et Crocodile Bridge, dans la zone centrale et au nord du fleuve Olifants. Un large troupeau (les seuls survivants des buffles du sud de la province du Cap) est protégé dans le Parc National Addo des Éléphants. Dans le Parc National Kruger, la femelle met bas un seul petit, généralement entre janvier et avril.

Poids du mâle	800 kg
Hauteur au garrot	140 cm
Vitesse sur courte distance	50 km/h
Écartement record des cornes	125 cm
Longévité	25 ans
Durée de la gestation	11 mois

**KRUGER/
ADDO**

AFRIKANISCHER BÜFFEL *Syncerus caffer*

Der Büffel kommt in weiten Gebieten des Kruger Nationalparks vor, besonders häufig zwischen Lower Sabie und Crocodile Bridge, sowie in der Mitte des Parks nördlich des Olifantflusses. Eine große Herde (die einzigen überlebenden Büffel in der südlichen Kapprovinz) kommt im Addo·Elephant Nationalpark vor. Im Kruger Nationalpark wird ein einziges Kalb gewöhnlich zwischen Januar und April geboren.

Gewicht (Männchen)	800 kg
Schulterhöhe	140 cm
Schnelligkeit über eine kurze Strecke	50 km/h
Rekordspannweite der Hörner	125 cm
Mögliche Lebensdauer	25 Jahre
Trächtigkeitszeit	11 Monate

**KRUGER/
ADDO**

VLAKHAAS *Lepus capensis*

Kom in die Nasionale Krugerwildtuin en talle ander nasionale parke voor. Dit woon nie in gate nie, maar kan in erdvark- of ander gate skuil wanneer bedreig. Gewoonlik word twee kleintjies per werpsel gebore.

Massa	2 kg
Lengte (met stert)	.45-60 cm
Moontlike lewensduur	.5-6 jaar
Draagtyd	42 dae

**KRUGER/
GOLDEN GATE/
BERGKWAGGA/
KAROO/
KALAHARI-GEMSBOK/
LANGEBAAN**

CAPE HARE *Lepus capensis*

Occurs in the Kruger National Park and in several other national parks. It does not live in burrows but may shelter in aardvark or other holes when threatened. Usually two young are born per litter.

Mass	2 kg
Length (with tail)	.45-60 cm
Potential longevity	5-6 years
Gestation period	42 days

**KRUGER/
GOLDEN GATE/
MOUNTAIN ZEBRA/
KAROO/
KALAHARI GEMSBOK/
LANGEBAAN**

LE LIÈVRE DU CAP *Lepus capensis*

On le rencontre dans le Parc National Kruger et dans plusieurs autres parcs nationaux. Il ne vit pas dans des terriers mais il s'abrite parfois dans les trous creusés par des oryctéropes (ou autres animaux) quand il est menacé. La femelle met généralement bas 2 petits par portée.

Poids	2 kg
Longueur (avec la queue)	.45-60 cm
Longévité	.5-6 ans
Durée de la gestation	42 jours

**KRUGER/
GOLDEN GATE/
ZÈBRE DE MONTAGNE/
KAROO/
KALAHARI GEMSBOK/
LANGEBAAN**

KAPHASE *Lepus capensis*

Der Kaphase kommt im Kruger Nationalpark und einigen anderen Nationalparks vor. Er lebt nicht in Bauen, kann aber in Löchern von Erdferkeln oder anderen Tieren Deckung suchen. Gewöhnlich werden 2 Junge pro Wurf geboren.

Gewicht	2 kg
Länge (mit Schwanz)	.45-60 cm
Mögliche Lebensdauer	5-6 Jahre
Trächtigkeitszeit	42 Tage

**KRUGER/
GOLDEN GATE/
MOUNTAIN ZEBRA/
KAROO/
KALAHARI GEMSBOK/
LANGEBAAN**

NATALSE ROOIHAAS *Pronolagus crassicaudatus*

Bewoon kranse en rotsagtige berghange in die Nasionale
Krugerwildtuin. Een of twee kleintjies word per werpsel
gebore, maar andersins is daar maar min bekend omtrent
die gewoontes van hierdie spesie.

Massa	2,5 kg
Lengte	50 cm
Draagtyd	1 maand

KRUGER

NATAL RED HARE *Pronolagus crassicaudatus*

Frequents kranses and rocky mountain slopes in the Kruger
National Park. One or two young are born per litter but
otherwise little is known about the habits of this species.

Mass	2,5 kg
Length	50 cm
Gestation period	1 month

KRUGER

LE LIÈVRE ROUGE DU NATAL *Pronolagus crassicaudatus*

Il fréquente les pentes rocailleuses du Parc National Kruger.
La femelle met bas 1 ou 2 petits. Les moeurs de cette
espèce sont pratiquement inconnues.

Poids	2,5 kg
Longueur	50 cm
Durée de la gestation	1 mois

KRUGER

NATALER ROTHASE *Pronolagus crassicaudatus*

Er lebt zwischen Felsen und an felsigen Berghängen im
Kruger Nationalpark. Ein oder 2 Junge werden pro Wurf
geboren, aber sonst ist wenig über dieses Tier bekannt.

Gewicht	2,5 kg
Länge	50 cm
Trächtigkeitszeit	1 Monat

KRUGER

KOLHAAS *Lepus saxatilis*

Hierdie spesie is baie soortgelyk aan die vlakhaas, maar verkies meer woudryke habitats met struikgewasse. Gewoonlik word 2 tot 3 kleintjies per werpsel gebore.

Massa	2,2 kg
Lengte	55 cm
Draagtyd	40 dae

**KRUGER/
GOLDEN GATE/
BERGKWAGGA/
ADDO/BONTEBOK/
KAROO/AUGRABIES/
KALAHARI-GEMSBOK/
LANGEBAAN**

SCRUB HARE *Lepus saxatilis*

This species is very similar to the Cape hare but favours habitats with more woodland and scrub cover. Usually 2 to 3 young are born per litter.

Mass	2,2 kg
Length	55 cm
Gestation period	40 days

**KRUGER/
GOLDEN GATE/
MOUNTAIN ZEBRA/
ADDO/BONTEBOK/
KAROO/AUGRABIES/
KALAHARI GEMSBOK/
LANGEBAAN**

LE LIÈVRE DE BROUSSE *Lepus saxatilis*

Cette espèce est très proche du lièvre du Cap mais il préfère des terrains plus boisés et arbustifs. La femelle met bas 2 ou 3 petits.

Poids	2,2 kg
Longueur	55 cm
Durée de la gestation	40 jours

**KRUGER/
BONTEBOK/
GOLDEN GATE/
ZÈBRE DE MONTAGNE/
ADDO/KAROO/AUGRABIES/
KALAHARI GEMSBOK/
LANGEBAAN**

FELDHASE *Lepus saxatilis*

Dieses Tier ist dem Kaphasen sehr ähnlich. Es bevorzugt aber Gebiete mit dichterem Pflanzenwuchs. Gewöhnlich werden 2 bis 3 Junge pro Wurf geboren.

Gewicht	2,2 kg
Länge	55 cm
Trächtigkeitszeit	40 Tage

**KRUGER/
GOLDEN GATE/
MOUNTAIN ZEBRA/
ADDO/BONTEBOK/
KAROO/AUGRABIES/
KALAHARI GEMSBOK/
LANGEBAAN**

YSTERVARK *Hystrix africaeaustralis*

Hierdie nagdier kom voor in die meeste van ons parke. Die rug en agterlyf is bedek met harde, skerp-puntige penne en die res van die liggaam met lang, stywe borselhare. Een tot 3 kleintjies word per werpsel gebore.

Massa	. . . . .17 kg
Lengte (met stert)	. . . . . 75-100 cm
Moontlike lewensduur	. . . . . 20 jaar
Draagtyd	. . . . 2 maande

**KRUGER/GOLDEN GATE/
BERGKWAGGA/
ADDO/TSITSIKAMMA/
BONTEBOK/KAROO/
KALAHARI-GEMSBOK/
LANGEBAAN**

PORCUPINE *Hystrix africaeaustralis*

The porcupine is nocturnal in habit and occurs in most of our national parks. The back and hindquarters are covered with hard, sharp-pointed quills, and the rest of the body with long stiff bristles. One to 3 young are born per litter.

Mass	. . . . 17 kg
Length (with tail)	. . . . . . 75-100 cm
Potential longevity	. . . . . . 20 years
Gestation period	. . . . . . 2 months

**KRUGER/GOLDEN GATE/
MOUNTAIN ZEBRA/
ADDO/TSITSIKAMMA/
BONTEBOK/KAROO/
KALAHARI GEMSBOK/
LANGEBAAN**

LE PORC-ÉPIC *Hystrix africaeaustralis*

Le porc-épic est un animal nocturne qu'on rencontre dans la plupart de nos parcs nationaux. Le dos et l'arrière-train sont recouverts de piquants longs et acérés et le reste du corps de long poils rigides. La femelle met bas de 1 à 3 petits.

Poids	. . . . .17 kg
Longueur (avec la queue)	. 75-100 cm
Longévité	. . . . 20 ans
Durée de la gestation	. . . . . . 2 mois

**KRUGER/GOLDEN GATE/
ZÈBRE DE MONTAGNE/
ADDO/TSITSIKAMMA/
BONTEBOK/KAROO/
KALAHARI GEMSBOK/
LANGEBAAN**

STACHELSCHWEIN *Hystrix africaeaustralis*

Das Stachelschwein ist ein Nachttier und kommt in den meisten unserer Nationalparks vor. Der Rücken und die Hinterteile des Tieres sind mit harten, scharfen, spitzen Stacheln bedeckt, und der Rest des Körpers wird durch lange, steife Borsten beschützt. Ein bis 3 Junge werden pro Wurf geboren.

Gewicht	. . . . .17 kg
Länge (mit Schwanz)	. . 75-100 cm
Mögliche Lebensdauer	. . . 20 Jahre
Trächtigkeitszeit	. . . . . . 2 Monate

**KRUGER/GOLDEN GATE/
MOUNTAIN ZEBRA/
ADDO/TSITSIKAMMA/
BONTEBOK/KAROO/
KALAHARI GEMSBOK/
LANGEBAAN**

BOOMEEKHORING *Paraxerus cepapi*

'n Boomdiertjie wat van insekte, blaarknoppies, vrugte, sade en bessies lewe. Gewoonlik word 1 tot 3 kleintjies per werpsel in hol boomstompe gebore.

Massa	.200 g
Lengte (met stert)	35 cm
Moontlike lewensduur	15 jaar
Draagtyd	55 dae

KRUGER

TREE SQUIRREL *Paraxerus cepapi*

An arboreal animal whose diet consists of insects, leaf-buds, fruit, seeds and berries. Usually 1 to 3 young are produced per litter, in holes in tree-trunks.

Mass	200 g
Length (with tail)	35 cm
Potential longevity	15 years
Gestation period	55 days

KRUGER

L'ÉCUREUIL DES ARBRES *Paraxerus cepapi*

Un animal arboricole qui se nourrit d'insectes, de bourgeons, de fruits, de graines et de baies. La femelle met généralement bas de 1 à 3 jeunes, qui naissent dans des trous dans des troncs d'arbres.

Poids	.200 g
Longueur (avec la queue)	35 cm
Longévité	15 ans
Durée de la gestation	55 jours

KRUGER

BAUMHÖRNCHEN *Paraxerus cepapi*

Ein Tier, das in Bäumen lebt, und das sich von Insekten, Blattknospen, Früchten, Samen und Beeren ernährt. Gewöhnlich werden ein bis 3 Junge in hohlen Baumstämmen geboren.

Gewicht	200 g
Länge (mit Schwanz)	35 cm
Mögliche Lebensdauer	15 Jahre
Trächtigkeitszeit	55 Tage

KRUGER

WAAIERSTERTMEERKAT *Xerus inauris*

'n Klein diertjie wat in droë parke soos die Kalahari-gemsbok Nasionale Park en die Bergkwagga Nasionale Park in gate woon. Dit vreet plante en sade en grawe wortels en bolle uit. Een tot 3 kleintjies word per werpsel gebore.

Massa	.650 g
Lengte (met stert)	45 cm
Moontlike lewensduur	15 jaar
Draagtyd	45 dae

BERGKWAGGA/
KAROO/
AUGRABIES/
KALAHARI-GEMSBOK

GROUND SQUIRREL *Xerus inauris*

A small animal which inhabits the drier parks such as the Kalahari Gemsbok National Park and Mountain Zebra National Park. Lives in burrows. Feeds on plants and seeds and digs up roots and bulbs. One to 3 young are born per litter.

Mass	650 g
Length (with tail)	45 cm
Potential longevity	15 years
Gestation period	45 days

MOUNTAIN ZEBRA/
KAROO/
AUGRABIES/
KALAHARI GEMSBOK

L'ÉCUREUIL TERRESTRE *Xerus inauris*

C'est un petit animal que l'on trouve dans les parcs plus secs comme les parcs nationaux Kalahari gemsbok et Zèbre de Montagne. Il vit dans des terriers. Il se nourrit de plantes et de graines et déterre des racines et des bulbes. La femelle met bas de 1 à 3 petits.

Poids	.650 g
Longueur (avec la queue)	45 cm
Longévité	15 ans
Durée de la gestation	45 jours

ZÈBRE DE MONTAGNE/
KAROO/
AUGRABIES/
KALAHARI GEMSBOK

BORSTENHÖRNCHEN *Xerus inauris*

Ein kleines Tier, das in den trockenen Parks wie im Kalahari Gemsbok- und im Mountain Zebra Nationalpark vorkommt. Es lebt in Bauen und ernährt sich von Pflanzen und Samen. Es gräbt auch Wurzeln und Knollen aus. Ein bis 3 Junge werden pro Wurf geboren.

Gewicht	.650 g
Länge (mit Schwanz)	45 cm
Mögliche Lebensdauer	15 Jahre
Trächtigkeitszeit	45 Tage

MOUNTAIN ZEBRA/
KAROO/
AUGRABIES/
KALAHARI GEMSBOK

SPRINGHAAS *Pedetes capensis*

Hierdie nagdier bly bedags in gate. 'n Enkele kleintjie word gewoonlik gebore, maar soms word twee gebore.

Massa	3 kg
Lengte (met stert)	80 cm
Moontlike lewensduur	7,5 jaar
Draagtyd	45 dae

**KRUGER/
GOLDEN GATE/
BERGKWAGGA/
ADDO/
AUGRABIES/
KALAHARI-GEMSBOK**

SPRING-HARE *Pedetes capensis*

This is a nocturnal animal which hides in a burrow during the day-time. Females normally produce a single offspring but twins do occur now and again.

Mass	3 kg
Length (with tail)	80 cm
Potential longevity	7,5 years
Gestation period	45 days

**KRUGER/
GOLDEN GATE/
MOUNTAIN ZEBRA/
ADDO/
AUGRABIES/
KALAHARI GEMSBOK**

LE LIÈVRE SAUTEUR *Pedetes capensis*

C'est un animal nocturne qui passe la journée dans un terrier. Les femelles mettent généralement bas un seul jeune mais il arrive qu'elles aient des jumeaux.

Poids	3 kg
Longueur (avec la queue)	80 cm
Longévité	7,5 ans
Durée de la gestation	45 jours

**KRUGER/
GOLDEN GATE/
ZÈBRE DE MONTAGNE/
ADDO/
AUGRABIES/
KALAHARI GEMSBOK**

SPRINGHASE *Pedetes capensis*

Der Springhase ist ein Nachttier, das sich während des Tages in einem Bau versteckt. Meistens wird ein einzelnes Junges geboren, aber Zwillinge kommen hin und wieder vor.

Gewicht	3 kg
Länge (mit Schwanz)	80 cm
Mögliche Lebensdauer	7,5 Jahre
Trächtigkeitszeit	45 Tage

**KRUGER/
GOLDEN GATE/
MOUNTAIN ZEBRA/
ADDO/
AUGRABIES/
KALAHARI GEMSBOK**

SEESOOGDIERE

Ons tref vandag vier groepe soogdiere aan wat by 'n lewe in die see aangepas het, nl. die see-otters van die Noord-Amerikaanse kus, die manatees en dugongs van die Ou en Nuwe wêrelde, die robbe, en die walvisse. Die robbe en walvisse (insluitende die dolfyne) word goed in Suid-Afrikaanse waters verteenwoordig en verskeie spesies kan by die Tsitsikammaseekus Nasionale Park gesien word. Ons enigste inwonende rob is die Kaapse pelsrob *(Arctocephalus pusillus)*. Dit kom in ongeveer 23 broei-kolonies voor vanaf Suidwes-Afrika/Namibië tot Algoabaai.

Massa (bul)	190 kg
Lengte (bul)	2,2 m
Massa (koei)	75 kg
Lengte (koei)	1,6 m
Draagtyd	1 jaar

MARINE MAMMALS

Four groups of mammals have adapted to life in the sea. These are the sea-otters of the North American coast, the manatees and dugongs of the Old and New Worlds, the seals, and the whales. The seals and whales (including the dolphins) are well represented in South African waters and several species can be seen off the Tsitsikamma Coastal National Park. Our only resident seal is the Cape fur-seal *(Arctocephalus pusillus)*, an eared seal related to the sea-lions of the Pacific Ocean. It occurs in 23 breeding colonies from South West Africa/Namibia to Algoa Bay.

Mass (male)	190 kg
Length (male)	2,2 m
Mass (female)	75 kg
Length (female)	1,6 m
Gestation period	1 year

LES MAMMIFÈRES MARINS

Quatre groupes de mammifères se sont adaptés au milieu aquatique: les loutres marines de la côte nord-américaine, les lamantins et dugongs d'Europe et d'Amérique, les phoques et les baleines. Les phoques et les baleines (y compris les dauphins) sont très répandus dans les eaux sud-africaines et plusieurs espèces sont visibles dans le Parc National de la Côte de Tsitsikamma. La seule otarie sud-africaine est l'otarie à fourrure du Cap *(Arctocephalus pusillus)*. On la rencontre dans environ 23 colonies de reproduction, de la Namibie à Algoa Bay.

Poids du mâle	190 kg
Longueur du mâle	2,2 m
Poids de la femelle	75 kg
Longueur de la femelle	1,6 m
Durée de la gestation	1 an

IN MEER LEBENDE SÄUGETIERE

Vier Säugetiergruppen haben sich den Lebensbedingungen im Meer angepaßt: die Seeotter an der nordamerikanischen Küste, die Manatis und Dugongs der Alten und Neuen Welt, die Robben und die Wale. Es gibt viele Robben und Wale (einschließlich der Delphine) in den südafrikanischen Küstengewässern, und an der Küste im Tsitsikamma Coastal Nationalpark können mehrere Arten beobachtet werden. Unsere einzige Standrobbe ist die Kapsche Pelzrobbe *(Arctocephalus pusillus)*. Sie kommt in etwa 23 Herden von Südwestafrika/Namibia bis Algoa Bay vor.

Gewicht (Männchen)	190 kg
Länge (Männchen)	2,2 m
Gewicht (Weibchen)	75 kg
Länge (Weibchen)	1,6 m
Trächtigkeitszeit	1 Jahr

DOLFYNE

Dolfyne maak 'n afsonderlike familie van die getande walvisse uit en 19 spesies is al in Suider-Afrikaanse waters opgeteken. Vyf van die mees algemene spesies word hier beskryf, en mag langs die strande van die Tsitsikammaseekus Nasionale Park voorkom. Dit is baie moeilik om hulle op see te onderskei. Die langvin-loodswalvis is die grootste, met 'n lengte van 6 meter, terwyl die ander tussen 2 en 3 meter lank is.
Illustrasies (links na regs, bo tot onder):

1. **Streepdolfyn** (*Stenella coeruleoalba*)
2. **Gewone dolfyn** (*Delphinus delphis*)
3. **Boggelrugdolfyn** (*Sousa plumbea*)
4. **Indiese Oseaan-stompneusdolfyn** (*Tursiops aduncus*)
5. **Langvinloodswalvis** (*Globicephala melaena*)

DOLPHINS

Dolphins form a distinct family of the toothed whales and 19 species have been recorded from southern African waters. Five of the commonest species are illustrated here, and may be seen off the shores of the Tsitsikamma Coastal National Park. They are very difficult to distinguish at sea. The long-finned pilot whale is the largest with a length of 6 metres, the other four being between 2 and 3 metres long.
Illustrations (left to right, top to bottom):

1. **Striped dolphin** (*Stenella coeruleoalba*)
2. **Common dolphin** (*Delphinus delphis*)
3. **Humpback dolphin** (*Sousa plumbea*)
4. **Indian Ocean bottlenosed dolphin** (*Tursiops aduncus*)
5. **Long-finned pilot whale** (*Globicephala melaena*)

LES DELPHINIDÉS

Les dauphins forment une famille particulière dans l'ordre des baleines à dents. On en a enregistré dix-neuf espèces dans les eaux sud-africaines. Cinq des espèces les plus communes sont illustrées, qui sont visibles au large du Parc National de la Côte de Tsitsikamma. Elles sont malaisées à distinguer en mer. La baleine à longue nageoire est la plus grande (six mètres de longueur); les quatres autres font entre deux et trois mètres de longueur.
Illustrations (de gauche à droite et de haut en bas)

1. **Le dauphin à rayures** (*Stenella coeruleoalba*)
2. **Le dauphin commun** (*Delphinus delphis*)
3. **Le dauphin à bosse** (*Sousa plumbea*)
4. **Le dauphin souffleur de l'océan indien** (*Tursiops aduncus*)
5. **La baleine à longue nageoire** (*Globicephala melaena*)

DELPHINE

Die Delphine gehören zur Familie der Zahnwale. In südafrikanischen Gewässern sind 19 Delphinarten verzeichnet worden. Fünf der am häufigsten vorkommenden Arten, die an der Küste des Tsitsikamma Coastal Nationalparks gesichtet werden können, sind abgebildet. Es ist sehr schwierig, sie im Meer zu unterscheiden. Der Langflossenpilotwal ist das größte Tier mit einer Länge von 6 m, während die anderen vier eine Länge von zwischen 2 und 3 m erreichen. Abbildungen (von links nach rechts, von oben nach unten):

1. **Gestreifter Delphin** (*Stenella coeruleoalba*)
2. **Gemeiner Delphin** (*Delphinus delphis*)
3. **Buckeldelphin** (*Sousa plumbea*)
4. **Indischer-Ozean-Küstendelphin** (*Tursiops aduncus*)
5. **Langflossenpilotwal** (*Globicephala melaena*)

WALVISSE

Agt spesies van die baard- of baleinwalvisse is al in
Suider-Afrikaanse waters opgeteken. Hierdie walvisse vreet
klein mariene organismes wat hulle in die water filtreer deur
'n delikate ineengeslote netwerk van groot baleinplate in hul
bekke. Al drie spesies van die potvis is ook al in ons
kuswaters opgeteken. Die grootste is die potvis self wat
meestal van diepwater-inkvisse lewe. Die afbeeldings hier
oorkant is van drie van die baleinwalvisse wat moontlik by
die Tsitsikammaseekus Nasionale Park gesien kan word,
asook die potvis. Hulle is:

1. **Boggelwalvis** (*Megaptera novaeangliae*)
2. **Suidelike noordkaper** (*Balaena glacialis*)
3. **Potvis** (*Physeter macrocephalus*)
4. **Vinwalvis** (*Balaenoptera physalus*)

WHALES

Eight species of baleen whales have been recorded from
South African waters. These whales eat small marine
organisms which they strain from the water through the fine
interlocking mesh of the great plates of baleen (or 'whale-
bone') in their mouths. All three species of sperm whale
have also been recorded from our coastal waters. The
largest is the sperm whale itself which feeds mostly on deep-
water squids. The illustrations opposite show three of the
baleen whales likely to be seen off the Tsitsikamma Coastal
National Park, as well as the sperm whale. They are:

1. **Humpback whale** (*Megaptera novaeangliae*)
2. **Southern right whale** (*Balaena glacialis*)
3. **Sperm whale** (*Physeter macrocephalus*)
4. **Fin whale** (*Balaenoptera physalus*)

LES BALEINES

On a enregistré huit espèces de baleines à fanons dans les
eaux sud-africaines. Elles se nourrissent de petits
organismes marins qu'elles filtrent au travers des mailles qui
constituent les fanons présents dans leur bouche. On a
également noté la présence des trois espèces de cachalots
au large des côtes sud-africaines. La nourriture du grand
cachalot se compose principalement de calmars. Les
illustrations ci-contre représentent trois des baleines à
fanons les plus susceptibles d'être vues au large de la côte
de Tsitsikamma, ainsi que le cachalot.

1. **La baleine à bosse** (*Megaptera novaeangliae*)
2. **La baleine franche** (*Balaena glacialis*)
3. **Le cachalot** (*Physeter macrocephalus*)
4. **Le rorqual commun** (*Balaenoptera physalus*)

WALE

Acht Walarten sind in südafrikanischen Gewässern
verzeichnet worden. Die Wale tragen lange Hornplatten
(Barten) mit daran befestigten borstenartigen Fasern, die
beim Schließen des Rachens wie ein Sieb die als Nahrung
dienenden kleinen Meerestiere zurückhalten. Alle drei
Pottwalarten sind auch in unseren Küstengewässern
verzeichnet worden. Die größte Art ist der Pottwal selbst,
der sich meistens von Tiefseetintenfischen nährt. Die
Abbildungen auf der nächsten Seite zeigen den Pottwal und
drei Bartenwalarten, die vom Tsitsikamma Coastal
Nationalpark aus beobachtet werden können.

1. **Buckelwal** (*Megaptera novaeangliae*)
2. **Südwal** (*Balaena glacialis*)
3. **Pottwal** (*Physeter macrocephalus*)
4. **Finnwal** (*Balaenoptera physalus*)

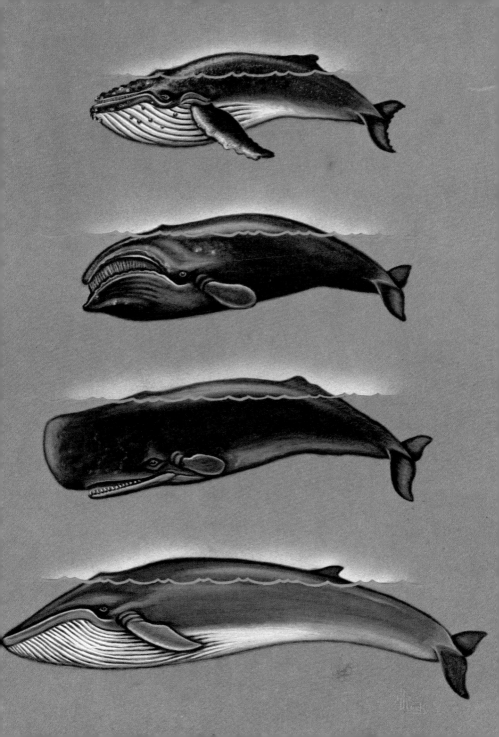